David Wevill

Collected Later Poems

By David Wevill

Penguin Modern Poets 4 (with David Holbrook & Christopher Middleton,
                                              Penguin Books, 1963)
Birth of a Shark (Macmillan / St. Martin's Press, 1964)
A Christ of the Ice-Floes (Macmillan / St. Martin's Press, 1966; Tavern Books, 2016)
Firebreak (Macmillan / St. Martin's Press, 1971)
Where the Arrow Falls (Macmillan, 1973; St. Martin's Press, 1974; Tavern Books, 2016)
Casual Ties (Curbstone, 1983; Tavern Books, 2010; Shearsman Books, 2022)
Other Names for the Heart: New & Selected Poems 1964–1984 (Exile Editions, 1985)
Figure of Eight: New Poems and Selected Translations (Exile Editions, 1987)
Figure of Eight (chapbook; Shearsman Books, 1988)
Child Eating Snow (Exile Editions, 1994)
Solo With Grazing Deer (Exile Editions, 2001)
Departures: Selected Poems (Shearsman Books, 2003; 2nd edition, 2013)
Asterisks (Exile Editions, 2007)
To Build My Shadow a Fire: The Poetry and Translations of David Wevill
    (edited by Michael McGriff, Truman State University Press, 2010)
Collected Earlier Poems (Shearsman Books, 2022)

As translator:
Selected Poems of Ferenc Juhász (with *Selected Poems of Sándor Weöres*,
                    translated by Edwin Morgan, Penguin Books, 1970)
Collected Translations (Tavern Books, 2014)
Translations (Shearsman Books, 2022)
Selected Poems of Ferenc Juhász (Shearsman Books, 2022)

David Wevill

Collected Later Poems

1974–2021

Shearsman Books

First published in the United Kingdom in 2022 by
Shearsman Books Ltd
PO Box 4239
Swindon
SN3 9FN

Shearsman Books Ltd Registered Office
30–31 St. James Place, Mangotsfield, Bristol BS16 9JB
(this address not for correspondence)

ISBN 978-1-84861-816-9

Copyright © David Wevill, 1985, 1987, 1994, 2001, 2007, 2022

The right of David Wevill to be identified as the author of this work has been asserted by him in accordance with the Copyrights, Designs and Patents Act of 1988. All rights reserved.

Acknowledgements

Three of the uncollected poems at the end of the volume first appeared in the online *Festschrift for Tony Frazer*, and all also appeared in *Exile* magazine, Toronto.

All the other poems were previously published in the following books:

Other Names for the Heart: New & Selected Poems 1964–1984
(Toronto: Exile Editions, 1985)

Figure of Eight: New Poems and Selected Translations
(Toronto: Exile Editions, 1987)

Child Eating Snow
(Toronto: Exile Editions, 1994)

Solo With Grazing Deer
(Toronto: Exile Editions, 2001)

Asterisks
(Toronto: Exile Editions, 2007)

Contents

Villa Blanca: Rincones and Other Poems
(1974-81)

Con Ansias	15
Spain	16
Rincón of the heady abstractions	17
Rincón for Paco the Fool	19
Rincón for the face in hotels	20
Rincón of the soon to be gone	21
Grace	23
The Unapproachable	24
Redtails	26
Late Sonnet V	27
Late Sonnet VIII	28
Shallots	29
Late Sonnet XII	30
Polonaise	31
The Dark Night	32
Like a Dog	34
Bolsón de Mapimi	35
Scavenging	37
Villa Blanca	38

Other Names for the Heart
(1981-85)

Child Sketch in Crayon	43
Visitors	45
Animula	46
Germinal	48
Snow Country	51
Formalities	54

Her Seasons	55
Other Names for the Heart	58
Landmarks	60
Childhood	61
A Story of Colors	62
Neutrons	64
Lovers	65
Cante Hondo	67
March Tilling	68
Words for Orpheus	69
The Conquest	72
Inktonmi, A Prayer	73
Paracentric	74
The Text	76

Figure of Eight
(1987)

Making Plans	81

Figure of Eight

Premonition	85
Figure of Eight	87

A Perfect Stranger

Interstice	105
Patterns Leaves Make	106
Why Distance is Necessary	107
Minima	108
Inhabitant	109
Chinese White	110
Primitive	112

Proof of How It Should Look	113
The Gift	115
Spain and Kafka	116
Soleá	118
Multiples	120
And Language is Everything	122
Andalusian Spring	123
The Village	124
Assia	125
Climbing	126
Homecoming	128
Black Glass	129
Full Moon Story	131

Child Eating Snow
(1994)

Baby Upside Down in a Light Snowfall	145
Blue Fur Hood	146
Christopher	147
Fugitives	148
Madame Matisse, 'The Green Line', 1905	149
Migrations	150
Child Eating Snow	151
Moving On, and With a Glance at Rilke	154
Exuberance (Paul Klee)	156
Separation in the Evening (Paul Klee, 1922)	157
Couplets, Late September	158
The Structure of the Ground	159
Paris, 1957	160
Then	161
Poem Depending on Dashes	162
Jeanne d'Arc	163

Jeanne d'Arc (2)	164
Jeanne d'Arc (3)	165
Ethnic Poem	166
Namelessness	167
Old Legends	168
A Thought from Yeats	169
Annunciation	170
Where the Soul Goes in Summer	171
Love Poem	172
Things That Can't Speak	173
Ethnic Poem II	175
A Man I Once Knew	176
The Long Semesters	177
From a Painting by Munch	178
Home Improvement	180
Le Sacre	181
Abstract	183
Old Age	184
Night Bus South	185
Altiplano	186
The Mystery	187
Daylight Saving	188
On a Monday in April	189
April, a Memo	190
Chelmno, Poland, Winter 1941	191
Beyond	192
New Year's Day Wedding	193
Yellow Flowers Out in January	194
Tortoise Shell	195
Old Families	196
Ethnic Poem III	197
Old Teacher	198
A Window in London	199
Bad Ghosts	200
Saeta	201

Night Clouds	202
Elzbieta	203
Three Daughters	204
Vigil	205
Above the Mediterranean	206
Montserrat	207
La Vida	208
Citlanicue (Star Mother)	209
Tlalteuctli (Earth Lady)	210
An Event About to Happen	211
Bettelheim	212
Soltera	213
Spirit	214
Ethnic Poem IV	215
Summer Storms	216
Trespassers	217
Those Childish Sundays	218
In Late June	219
Primo Levi	220
Chihuahua	221
Conversation	222
Fragment	223
Possession	224
Energy	225
Heatwave	226
Ethnic Poem V	227
Ottawa, April 1964	228
Poet's Poet	229
South Wind	230
Genesis	231
Wait	232
The Cemetery of the Nameless	233
Pied Piper	236
My Father's Hand	237
Summer Morning for Felicity	238

Solo with Grazing Deer
(2001)

The River That Drowned	241
Lamp	242
Sabi	244
Memory and Season	245
Rune	246
The High Cold Air	247
Landscape	248
Revenant	250
May Month	251
Blue Roofs	252
Caravans	253
ᛉ	255
Piscean Song	256
Stump	257
Railroad Tracks, House for Sale and Clouds	258
Happiness	259
February	260
Postcard	261
Soft Voices	262
The Intimacy of Distance	263
Winter	264
Granddaughter	265
San Michele, Venice	266
Force and Shadow	267
Memo	268
News Fragment	269
Reading Late	270
Illegals	271
Friday Thirteenth	272
Territory	274
Gernika	275
Winter Grass on the Plains	276

Late Night Movie	277
Wild Eyes	278
Frictions	279
How the Elderly Are Born	280
Sunlight Through Blinds,	
Four o'Clock, Facing West	281
Bethlehem	282
Incarnations	283
It Happens	284
Watermarks	287
Apples and Apples	289
Nocturne	291
Call Notes	293
Impression	294
Lucky Numbers	296
Of Magic	298
Not There Yet, Nowhere Near	299
Lifelines	301
High Winds and Heavy Snows	303
Memo	304
The Colour of Rocks, of Bread	306
Answers	308
Master of Wind	310
Vanished Numbers	311
Seed, Light	313
Fugitives	314
Man Carrying a Suitcase	315
Eyes	316
Departures	318
Histories	319
Wind	321
New Year	322
Cat and Mouse	324
Lights Across the Lake	326
Scattering	327

Time Out	330
Gathering	331
Vegetation	333
Spring 2001	335
Book Closing	337
Solo with Grazing Deer	338
The Naming of Absence	339

Asterisks (2007)   341

Uncollected Poems

Breath	397
Compassion	398
Autumnal	399
Winter	400
1918	401
Western Light	402
Introit	403
Birds	404
Past Tense	405

Notes on the Poems   407

Original cover texts   408

VILLA BLANCA

RINCONES & OTHER POEMS

1974–1981

Con Ansias

(For Alberto de Lacerda)

Burning nights ... Juan de la Cruz
escaping from the cell in Toledo
down the wall, into the arms
of the friendly sisters ... read his poems

aloud as the chain
ate into his flesh. Praised even the fishes
the harshness of summers at
high altitudes. Desire to give back

to his maker the unwanted body, corpus, corpse
mutilated later by the teeth and hands
of worshipers. An arm and a leg

as relics, the rest enshrined elsewhere.
For one moment of love in the garden with his beloved.
Desire the rushing of water under stones.

Spain

North wind at stalemate with the sun. Acorns
dropping where the wind has touched the oak tree.

You spent too much time living others' lives
Casually, as if detached from them. You've

earned the silence you wanted. Now
listen to the replay ... broken glass

underfoot across the red tile floor
of an abandoned police barracks high above the sea.

There is no entry point
no exit wound. But to come here now and think

why such stress still flickers about us like thin rain
the victims dead and gone. You held your sex

like a bouquet of lilies, close to your face.
You gave yourself away at noon like a bride.

Rincón of the heady abstractions

Densities: a summer in the country
like other summers in towns
measured by one light or another
that comes or refuses
reek of old earth. This

corner has no exit. If I remember
it is satisfaction of remembering & not
even a body or face to go
under for, strings in my hand
vibrating still with earth's winds.

Orpheus is too old to meet his question.
Above & below there are greater
certainties than love
remembered, a person. Blood
hardened like an old cat after many wars
now stretched out asleep in the sun.

In the country we learn silence
but among friends we are too talkative,
our gossip is old, what
news we must invent. We are painkillers.
We kill for pain & kill the pain
of those things we kill.

In towns this summer the country becomes
whatever age it wants to feel:
the spirit of independence, freed
by choice to choose lies. Lakes
edged by spruce & fir will always be backgrounds.

What happens up close is the perigee
of insatiable alternatives. One by one

they cut the strings of the song
& the song's replaced by noises that create
their own winds. In this garden
in this slum

we return to ourselves again
in memory. Where have they gone
the man & the woman who fled
terrified before the fiery angel & had

to learn to build fires & make new words
for things they couldn't love.
They were our type, not noble or heroic but
pressed to keep what they'd lost,
remake it with hands, in the smallest possible
image, themselves. & this

corner has no exit. Remembering
may seem one but is false, false
densities, narcosis of sounds of words in
summer thunder. Measured by the old light
one is pale as a fish & not yet
born. & those who confuse their times
remember nothing but what it is like not to be.

Rincón for Paco the Fool

If you grunt you will be understood
to be hungry, but the earth's
lost music is different.

He who walks with the men in the funeral march
& holds the tail of the mule
going downhill
is happy.

But pointing to your genitals
when a woman passes, is more than hunger
& who can tell you that.
Not the children with stones.

Those of us with voices are
trying, trying
but the nights devour our shadows leaving us
nowhere to meet you.

Sounds. You haven't one word
to catch us with.
But the earth's lost music is different
it is more restless.

I've gone up into the sky my face hangs there
watching for you.

Rincón for the face in hotels

Madrid in the rain. Every day
the same fool in the window
mutters 'water'.

One wind then two
searches the black afternoon light
in the museo del prado.
Yes yes there's been trouble
why did you come.

The black wind & the white wind
two horses pulling a star
it can be fatal

shapes drifting in rain from the mountains
colors drifting in rain from the mountains
mothers fathers names

but on wet days the goats
trot among the umbrellas
along paths near the glass conservatory
goats with eyes like fish.

Northward to Burgos the road
goes up & up breaking through cloud into France
a map of dark colors. The same
story begins to plan
its escape to a better one

some thing with too long a stride
that passed this way crushing people & rocks
all running except one donkey who
won't move.

Rincón of the soon to be gone

(For David Moorman)

Banded together again
here, in our now grassless yard –
the rough winterworn brown of occasions
like this – we talk
of unwritten poems, & the earth turns,
minute animations of friable soil
shaken by chainsaws. Wind
parts the cedars, & we imagine the deer
no longer with us, grass gone to the sun,
fencelines opening & closing
restlessly, as strangers make their plans
& are heard of or never appear except
a few more trees have gone. You
our old friend, familiar with the
guest room: this is your house too
where nerves can rest, though ours
aren't easy now & the place
has got out of hand –
unimaginable repairs & so little time
even for these words. We wish we knew how
to be inert & at peace, or
leap those fences & heal them with energy,
that light successful touch no thing can feel
when properly mended. We sit
here where our shadows have always lived
& talk. Soon one must move, some
story begin, arbitrarily, at its first word
& continue on as the wind takes it
faithful to its helplessness without
the signature of the oak or periwinkle
to guide it. So it will
go. It is spring, yet there's this

autumnal drift backward seven years
to a time of more credible waiting
for that war to end which is now just beginning –
blood, then & now, human
red or sap green: the old infection of choice
the same, the ways
both more open & closed. This is
peacetime, we tell ourselves. A time
for children or for lonely energies
to happen in themselves. The tree buds are
still hidden, uncertain: as in dreams
the clues keep generating new darknesses
we stumble on. The horizon of going
is never real enough, but many
pass into eclipse as talk leads us there
& beyond. Somewhere far away
in a city whose streets happen in memory
a table is being laid for your meal tonight.

Grace

(For Jim & Cara)

I imagined silence was a way of speaking
but it only returns to itself
asking for water. The way they sunned themselves
in each other's shadow, ripening too quickly

in talk too intimate
to carry this far. Are we not made naked
by others' desires? Otherwise why do the mountains
crowd us like a great bed filled with

everything imaginable and alive,
thing and not thing, probing
for openings to our hearts. Her long loose hair

smelling of smoke, drifting like smoke up
from the open firepit. A
whole country in someone's blackened thumbnail.

The Unapproachable

...the vague, the particular no less vague...
                —William Carlos Williams

The cure as with a flower is to water the root,
be gentle, precise in whatever you
can afford to give, what it wants.
The crown of lights it resembles are offices
far into the night
                      numbers giving birth
to new images of the future surrounding you,
and the bridge, the between, stretched
precariously tight from half
to half of what wholeness. Yet

the sun has never watched us,
nor the moon.
Paul Klee lowered the stars
until they hung too huge above our simple roofs,
and a woman turning to a man returns his key
with thanks but regrets. How grave the time would seem
without the jokes we're forced to make of ourselves
suspended like this, as we are,
searching the floor for a lost eye
without which it is hard for me to see
your hurt.
                    And the elevators dream

of going beyond, of lifting themselves high
above the layers of rain, or plummeting down
below the water-thirst of flowers
                    which in your hand
are ghostly smells, colors the night can't give
to anything other than numbers on a screen

as we, to meet ourselves, approach
a mirror placed to make the room seem larger
and are suddenly caught in a smile
both true and false, as the light changes
subtly like a deer running through woods,
but reminding us of blood, and how we tremble now.

Redtails

Always the search for a form
that doesn't resist. That
gesture of both greeting and farewell
perfectly ambiguous, perfectly true

which stops the clock. The sun sets
on the westward cliff, with or without movement of animals

straying through the grass. This is
halfway home, you think
halfway, but why? The ghost of a lyric in a

housefly's wings, the vanished hawks
take only a moment. Is it energy you're wanting but who
can tell us the way, the place?
Outnumbered by suns, by moons

what tower do you climb to fantasize your shadow.

Late Sonnet V

Virtually nothing is whole. I imitate myself in the mirror
combing someone else's hair.
Mornings devoted to traffic begin to seem

like an old path to the village well
whose pure water darkened
for no reason. I try
and the trying tastes bitter. Children

sacrificed at the edge of the well
left their names for others to find like
pebbles and string as necklaces. This

morning you walk out beautifully
to meet what calls you, not by name.

The necklace of stones you wear are my possible lives.

Late Sonnet VIII

Always suspect the stranger
but give him a roof, a bed, whatever he needs
to cut your firewood. Offer him blood to drink
and he'll open his heart

to the story you were telling
when he entered. In the firelight his eyes
remember: the autumn nights were cold.
The woods grew shadows no light could open.

He watches the firelight play on her arms
like shadows in a brown stream. The
house had no mood. Sometimes lately

a bird you can't identify has flitted close
and sung from the branches of his hands.

He leaves us touching ourselves.

Shallots

She dreamt
her tongue was made of mud.
When she spoke
the little shell-like syllables fell apart
as her tongue dissolved, no one
understood her. In the rain

her eyes stood as two pools
where someone's fingers had poked holes
and left them for the tide to fill.

Now
her children wonder where their mother went.
They finger their eyelids tentatively and
curl their tongues in the soft earth of speech

and breathe quickly, like children treading water.

Late Sonnet XII

Then seeing it was still alive
we put it in a jar where we could watch it
day and night. Wind and the seasonal rains
browned out the hills, staring through glass

the world seemed to grow older, grew
its colors inward, the beauty there
but gone. I read my daughter's essay and noted
a gift for heightened feeling expressed

as a wish to see us as we'd like to be
angels carved from driftwood
smelling of bodies in love. Delicately the light

steps over us who are
temporarily fallen. When we get up again
we leave these shadows as reminders of where we have been.

Polonaise

We drink the rain.
We open in the sun
but between these there are weeks of darkness
or hours when the light dries us

to a tense whisper. My blood
left me and curled up under a stone
in the canyon bottom. Your walk
as you approach this shadow is innocent

but movement is never innocent, it
attracts things, the prickly pear
this effigy with pins stuck in its heart

which stands for patience. We
don't go back there anymore. I wonder how they felt
waiting in line to be shot while the wind just stood there.

The Dark Night
—*San Juan de la Cruz*

On a dark night
love's anguish burning in me
o blessed risk
I went out, no one saw me
the house now quiet and still

Safely in the dark
by the secret ladder, disguised
o blessed chance
hidden in the dark
my house now quiet and still

In the night blest with secrecy
for no one saw me
and my self saw nothing
led by no other light
but what burned in my heart to guide me

which led me on
more surely than the light of noon
to where someone waited
whom I knew intimately
in a place where no one came

O night that led me on
night more obliging than any dawn
o night bringing together
the lover and the loved one
the beloved transformed in the Lover

On my flowering breast
kept only and wholly for him
he lay sleeping
while I caressed him
fanned by breezes from the cedar trees

A breeze off the parapets,
then as I spread out his hair
with a hand light as air
he touched and hurt my neck,
and all my senses hung there

I stayed, I forgot myself
I laid my face against my Lover.
Everything stopped, my self
my cares behind me
among the lilies forgotten.

Like a Dog

That night we avoided you. A
figure came up the street
looking for help. But the night was

too dark, there was anger in the wind
the restlessness that in America
kills on sight. Now the rain is out walking

stepping from one hill to the other
avoiding your field. The energy we waste talking
when there are things to be done

such as talk. And hard for us to sleep
who wake in our separate beds
to the same dream of a bell tolling somewhere

and think of a goatherd lost in his own mountains
running his hands over stones and counting their names.

Bolsón de Mapimi

But the desert is always familiar, its
white beds of old lakes
retain the form of water we have drunk at repeatedly
crying for more. They are gone now. We come

in a time of dry paper written on by wind
dust devils like angry composers erasing the lines of notes
that sound wrong. Only among
the surprise of green rushes around a living spring
a house wren nesting, her song, fish in the pools
& butterflies, wind in harmony with grass, is there

a smell of the older garden, something
Chinese & appropriate to the perpetual
wind chimes of the spirit. But the tracks that lead away
frantic & determined disappear
into themselves. Follow them & you are gone, a

hazy figure sketched above the stunted cactus
talking to yourself, the words
dripping off you like sweat until finally
there is no language left, no source, but the wind
entering you & leaving, finally, your bones

which are at home here. You must get so close
to see life at all. You must stand quite still
to appreciate the heat & the tiny
noises it makes, the
life sign written on the shared skin of fire
you inhabit with these, invisibly & forever

looking for something elsewhere. The dry mountains around
offer nothing but a steeper vertical sameness,
no life, no rain. We take a photograph
& there we are & the mountains, smiling, somewhere, anywhere

alive & awake in the sun that shares
our joke for the moment. Love of the desert is old,
old as the sun. But you would look
for Icarus in the bones of the sea, not here, not
this close to the fire that eats itself & leaves

its meaning too plain. Our time
has come & gone & will come again
in the intellect of baked adobe & desert stone
we remember as a form more ancient than gardens
& return to now & water it, cautiously, with our bodies.

Scavenging

Winter vines running like flames
across dry hillside. We speak
of fires we must light, of sleep, like the ghost
of a dead woman who visits us only to go

backing out a door
which is all doors into darkness
words can't open. The remaining grapes are soft
and taste too sweet

like the eyes of asiatic orphans
left to contemplate too long, but we
pick and fill a sack with the best we can find

and return at night at the same steep angle
awake and thoughtful. I've lived
unnecessary lives fingering what comes to me late.

Villa Blanca

The dark table where my ancestors ate
is here with us. Two white dogs
guard the entrance to the patio
while the fire on the mountainside at night spreads toward us.

A day spent among birds. Dinner
is talk of another kind, soft ash, fatigue
& America tuned in. The roof is for stars,
the deep slope south & west is where the Pacific begins

beneath our shoulders. Like ones standing in water
we are the mountains. Tomorrow the same &
then home, cutting the fine edge of our journey
along exactly the same line, backward. To

go at last in whatever direction
time tells us, telling us nothing else we can
hear. You are my friends & we all matter greatly
to someone or some idea whose

hidden solitudes need our voices: fire, child or star
confers on us the permanence of the
passer-by, the ones who have been & are about to
leave this table in the mountains as

the fire spreads closer. My ancestors
have cleared away the plates & we're
tired, our words fail us. There will never be a
city here. Our words are too particular, our

ideas shaped by dead names & forms
that call us back to imaginary beginnings
whose pressures remind us of birth, of
these ones born again in us to serve us & dismiss us

into the question of nightfall & distance
murmuring "time". When we're alone tonight
we will have nothing to talk with but our bodies.
They are this geography, the sierra's superficial bones.

OTHER NAMES FOR THE HEART

1981–1984

Child Sketch in Crayon

Two trees in full leaf, one
with the mouth of an owl's nest
halfway up the trunk. On a field of grass

seven flowers stand in a row
red, yellow, blue. The sky is filled
with simplifications of blackbirds or crows

and an eighth flower now
tucked against the tree trunk hides itself.
Someone has slashed the tree

deeply near its base, and she left
the sky white so the birds could fly
or because she did not want to fill

that whole space where blue is infinite
and doesn't belong. Love
is practical, of things, a color, a form

at the edge of what's possible
crying not to be released or made
perfect, but held, held there where it holds

itself in its own arms
which is what sleep is
when your dreams do not threaten the sun

— to learn caution with age, but what
is the metaphor for
terror? That you have outlived

the self you thought weak
but precious
and now the hard frost

where eloquence imagined a thousand colors
plucking the wind

                    the eye is a wind

it rises, it dies
the shadow she left in the grass
refuses to move. You'd need a thousand years.

Visitors

(For Christopher Middleton)

Where there were houses there is grass.
What we missed were the shadows
the sun crackling off
painted metal. A few thin trees.

We say we miss that, but the
photographs had it wrong, the latest
evidence shows a family no one remembers
posed in front of a lake

before a low sun
cutting into their eyes.
The shadow of a tree just touches
the man's left shoulder. The woman

leans down to speak
to one of the two girls. The
dogs that run everywhere looking for water
left prints on the muddy valley floor

which have dried. Something went wrong
with the mathematics, with the camera.
There is nowhere to settle here.
Nothing to settle on.

I scrape a bent, rusty nail
on a stone, to see if the metal will shine.
They walk their ponies back up through the grass
that covers the hill. They do not look back.

Animula

> *We have all become people according to the
> measure in which we have loved people and
> have had occasion for loving.*
> —*Pasternak*

If in your confusion
you could have seen the future
as other than death, as
what it might have been
for your left hand to have begun
perfectly writing the characters
of an unknown language, older than memory

so that the sun, seen clearly as the sun
not just as light, broke
inside you, without the pain of fire
and you were made new, newer than
anything you could remember
ever, of your past

and the man beside you, the woman
beside me, were both one, one
like the deepest vowel, so
that life and death were one sound
and what you had done and what I had
not done seemed only the shame

and pity of uncompleted gestures,
then ... Ana, we asked
what happened to your friend?
My friend gave up.
Were you too difficult to love?

But there is no world without pain
without pain no world.

The inner sun
burns in Cancer

white cold flakes arrested in their
fall to earth. Body

is only body, warmth and cold
not opposites but of the same memory

appetites, the old old hunger
like a warning, like a star.

Mind feeds on mind. Then what is matter?
What are the earth signs? Mind feeds on flesh.
Its hunger enters dreams, it
prowls and resembles an animal
but is mind. To go
and not come back. To
go and not come back.
To go and not come back

I have no body.
I have no body's body.
I am neutral like the sea.

The sun touches this other face
which is your skin, your death.
Beyond this are
the uncanny possibilities of ignorance,
innocence, the sea-bird's cry heard
all night in the girl's ear
repeating and repeating her new name.

Germinal

The days make
silence seem
more rigorous. Perhaps

some inhabitant of
the chain of meaning, a
sudden shout into
a microphone

                is where

a stranded king comes home
is recognized and touched
by her, his people

whatever has waited
hoped, or given up hope.
And the joy of return
is like a phrase

                inaccurately remembered

but charged, as in Ovid's exile
with a cruder blood
than his own, than his
pleading with her

for silent tongues around him
so he would not seem
to himself a fool

too long, too soon
and cry for this change
and weep for that other change
which makes less sense

which made no sense at all.

Between women and men
sometimes the same
mouth speaks. The

pleasures of touch, lips
eyelids, pubic hair
are how one lives again
as blood grows older

tormenting the salmon
we imagine
are happy to bear and die
each year

                for the sake of

time itself. But how
slowly silently the nerves
put out new shoots

kissed by the air, the sun
we had thought gone.
The days make
simply this

air. It is a bitter
reprieve, yet it smiles.
The life we keep
for want of living better

is precious. Could I have believed
the shout that broke my
poise, my silence

                    came from nowhere

but of itself
instinctive
cry into time, I would have

remembered birth
as this same moment, as
between us, the first look
ending this exile

this permanent dream
of self not happening. And
here, now, in the space

where the sleeping king wakes
gets up and walks
uphill, and the exiled poet

                    returns in his mind

to the lost world
of pain, and imagined pain
where she, and she
is the circle they

have chosen, is the heart
breaking into its body, the
old thief, the one of wholesome nerve.

Snow Country

(For Avanthi)

Kawabata talked about
the "roaring at the center"
deep in the mountains when snow
has covered them. This
is the sound of distances made
heavy, and bare of all details
between your blood and nothing.

Early in the day when things wake
listening, to be sure it is
the same world. And if
not, what power is there to make it
reappear (wind
is not a substance or
your breath on the mirror) the

picture you imagined,
come down to earth
like the angel in Tolstoy's story
to help you tie your shoes. A
child walks out the door you locked last night
and you hear yourself asking the time
in an empty house. It is

so important. Something to fill that
foot or so of space you're afraid
to leave. Why is it possible
to imitate almost anything but
oneself, the distance that listens
and has no answer? Because you dream at night
you are naïve

and nameless. Your helpless throat
drinks dust among sparrows.
Pretty soon, you say, pretty soon
I will look at you out of eyes
that have learned, in exile, how to fetch
things back, from that space between
a world I had composed

and this one which breaks me. Is it
that serious? Your
shadow like a pietà, limp in your arms
but carved hard in stone. There is
no voice at the center. But as
Ponge imagined it, "then the nocturnal
outcry reverberates", and

between your blood and nothing, in that space
where you were last seen alive
the mirror reforms, a fish swims at its edge
and amazes you. How many words does it take
to redeem one? The issue
is not love. That word is broken.
To wake up in the mountains, cold

with first snowfall, it could be memory
asking for food, a
child now adult gazing past herself into
the mirror of the wind, not lost
but patient. Your vision of being
at one with things is hard, not easy.
Your sense of being separate follows, it

resembles despair but can
still speak. When you leave
abruptly the door swings

like a body that can't decide
which way is out
and must guess its direction. Like Yoko's eyes
in the snow story, the girl whose body fell

dead through the flaming house, beyond words
or love. Only her leg
moved slightly. That is the feeling of silence
the cry at the center (not voice)
no one hears. You melt with the snow,
just the slightest pressure.
He lifts you up and takes you to the window

naked, to look at the white world
to look at the mountains.
This is the end, the departure, your
self from self, your substance from the mirror.
Distance takes your hand, the train comes in
leaving a sound of breaking glass.
Then the mountains, only the mountains.

Formalities

When someone is undressing she is naked before you see her nakedness. It is the figure's intention to undress that reveals her. You are watching and know the moment when her movement becomes stillness and the act is done. It is the moment of obsession when you recognize yourself in her, and your heart stops beating, your eyes turn into hands, and the hands are hers.

Her Seasons

Who you are not
is who you will never be

first the *breva*
then the fig
at different times
two different fruits
on the same tree

you are not like that

this figure cutting between two idling trucks
in a hurry to cross the road
disappears in someone's doorway
suddenly as the sun goes in
and the fig tree spreads its shadow over the earth
like a mind suddenly aware
it knows nothing at all

and that life changes
and you change, you change life
are not the same thing, the bird's
groin anoints, in
sunlight, her feathers
held by his beak, this
play of words between us

if we are to succeed

that which you are, becoming
what you are not
is not

quite possible

likelihood
is the force of the sun
multiplied by every thing
its hands have touched

do you want it to be this way
you forget, you forget
who you are, what
doorway you go into
a ship's horn following you like the cry
of a bull from the harbor its
gigantic cranes at rest

and all that hair

that fine intelligence
wearing its bright skirt
like a banner against the indignity
of having to explain
the fig tree's double life
its twice-bearing, twice-born
replica of the first fruit

this is not your life

the southern Mediterranean city
filled with otherness
streets of shadow, streets of sun
time hidden, time
deepening in gardens

it lifts us like smoke
over the green hedges of our birthplace
until we touch our first beds
and find them unmade

Other Names for the Heart

This feebleness, this trembling
at the edge of self. Robert

Schumann suffered fits
of shivering, apprehensions of death.

Fear of high places. Fear of all
metal instruments including keys.

The note A sounding always in his ears
later became voices. His

piano returned to the silence of wood.
The air that gave him music

reverted to air. Wind, and rain on the window.

What do you listen for? The earth
is wounded. Earth cannot make you whole.

Spirits of the old
earth return, yes, they
linger and confuse you. Yet we are bodies

and sometimes, when the light is good
we move as music, we compose ourselves
in patterns of exact time

and dance as blood to blood, the piano
silent, the melody only in ourselves.

But it takes the courage of gods
and we are human. It requires

what our eyes refuse to see
to see ourselves, as Schumann
dragged from the icy river, the Rhine
in February, quite insane

saw or
felt himself that night
breaking the surface, the cold flow
of time his hands had touched so masterfully.

Other names for the heart, all
obsessional, like the heart itself

rise like bubbles of air
the breath we keep or lose. Some boatmen

found him and pulled him to shore.
What they rescued was a question answered.

Landmarks

Turning
bitterly to the light
he asks
is this my father's face
are these my father's hands

and the light
spoke with her voice
how can I answer
I see nothing, nothing

but the figure of a twisted tree
on an empty hillside

it cries, it speaks
a language I have never understood.

Childhood

There comes a time when the habit of moving on
overcomes the sense of being in any place.

No destination is final, against
the finality of leaving or arriving.

This is when a child begins
hunting in mirrors for the smell of earth.

A Story of Colors

One dies. The other suffers. One is born.
There is a light they all mistook for
walking in the pine woods, above
a castle of pink stone. Or

rippling like squirrels after each others' tails
and the births of many children
followed by sleep. The light
turns, folds

into a *caracol* whose sea-shush ear
withholds their voices. "Why
can't we imagine transparent white glass"
she said. And he, "Imagine it." Her eyes

followed the storm line above the low mountains
up where the olives ended and the pines
began, a lighter green. "A color
shines in its surroundings. Just as eyes

only smile in a face." Then
the ghost between them flew away like birds
into the startling rain, for
shelter or fear. I don't know where

a story has its heart. Beginning
middle or end, the substance where the light
that shines from it breeds
words, or children. If at the very beginning

things die, and the suffering then
is to bear again the beginning, bring it to light
in the end, can the circle
move, be fruitful? Abelard

ringed like a tree
died at last. And she passed on
into the color grey, which doesn't shine.
Language inadequate without

the rise and fall of blood between
two bodies, the deepest fall
into black that absorbs all light.
One following the other, they picked their track

under the storm, the imagined pine woods
taking the light from their skin
the pinebark flickering like an illusion
of sacred fire, a welcome or a warning

of sacrifice. The philosopher on his walk
comes upon them, looks away and
passes on. And he is the one
who will suffer the memory of what he has seen

forever, his passion, compassion,
life, lived in praise of light, light's heart
broken in him by this accident. The eyes
are telltales only. They have not the power

to bring summer down from the hills,
to heal what grows cold. The days
wander like torches lost in the dark. They
waver, shine brilliantly, and almost lose heart.

Neutrons

When the wind blows
you often get this feeling
somewhere there is a city
that does not feel it

the city that is
not the citizens
who are part of the wind
who appear and disappear
like theorems on a blackboard

It might be
that up in the Generalife
among the cool, perfectly silent cedars
philosophers and mathematicians
meditating, talking among themselves
knew of this wind

The precise desert voice
returns to us now
as we stand high above the world
thinking of the tribes that will live
and those that will die

the numbers we call passion.

Lovers

Two settle to talk
at an outdoor table
their knees angled between
the straight metal legs
under the frosted glass
cones they drink from.

Laughter comes first
then silence. The sun
or her companion
makes her frown that way
and his diffidence draws
on other figures passing

uncertain conclusions
that gather as shadows around
the lily-like poise of her head
making the hour's history
catch up with and surround and
darken it, the

color now deep blue
as in the lemon sunlight
eyes play tricks. They are
nearing middle age now
and he reaches to touch her.
She's crying. But the forecast was for

dry weather, his sunburnt hand
withdraws in disbelief
and she settles herself again
and gazes out at the hills

that speak no language she knows
turning and turning

her empty glass
through which sand falls
in a thin stream like his voice
talking of other things. "Why
we came here and
where we go to now

is what keeps us here
stiff and helpless as the bones
we know we will leave for others
to find and puzzle over and
give names to, like the one
who was watching us and is gone

trailing his hand on the table
to show his reluctance
to leave or accompany us
one and one or two
on the long walk we must take
our separate ways he owns now."

Cante Hondo

At eighty-two her great artery
broke in the old woman. She
fell and they laid her out
on the white reddening bed.

Now after the funeral
the mattress and sheets are piled
at the back of the house.
Tomorrow

he will take them into the field
and light a match.
He will burn the blood of his mother.
No one else can do this.

March Tilling

(For S. L. W. (1910–1964)

Cancer aged her suddenly. She died
older than she might have looked
twenty years later. Now

it is twenty years later
and we are scattered, all three of us
with eight children among us
none of whom ever saw her.

This is where stories could help
but we never speak of her. The
photos are mostly lost, there is
no way to bring it through to this year's leaves

to ruckle up a name an
identity from the soil's stubborn
underside. The tiller bucks and shakes

just under the lip of first rain.
Roots catch in it, bamboo roots
flare yellow in the darkening light, and
I strain and strain. No time to stop it now.

Words for Orpheus

Now that you have become she
your face her face
your body hers

the change almost complete
the distance grows until it becomes
pure presence
but without

the details presence had
not needing to be remembered
as now

memory tries
and tries too hard
like a dog circling its permanent ache
for a place
to lie comfortably

I at my own heels
tread too close to recognize
the half of my body she left me

in the near total calm
of the cold November sun
struggle to get up
try to get back

to the meaning of this pattern of sheer loss
the words the voice changed
thin now, nerves only almost

to imagine a new face
perfect as an icon, but colorless
imprinted on air
which is the future's walls

always receding, always there
they take no shadow
they make no claim but

patience
which is not a virtue now
it being too much
a circling back
to what is impossible

that the voice chanting in the firelight
was the voice of a singer
and now the leaves will wait until

the first frost
which has touched us both already
changing the meanings of words
we learnt together

that grew too familiar
that became finally the bones
of an older love we had only borrowed
for a while
which we fleshed with ourselves

and now, how you have changed
how she has become that distance
that separates me from the critical sky

where the past walks in glory
backwards, like an omen in reverse
its hands outstretched to touch
something I cannot see
which has no human features

no mask, no name
so bright is the overwhelming sun
that blinds me and makes my blood cold.

The Conquest

I lean into the crowd and ask
who is it what happened

there are streaks of sky across a puddle
where sailing ships move
hinting at new discoveries

the beginning of a green coastline
fringed thinly with blood

and someone says
it was my mother it was my mother
but what happened
whose

voice is that singing the ave maria
repeatedly like a hungry animal

I watch and learn something
of the inconsistency of laughter
faced with sudden rain

Inktonmi, a Prayer

The companions of Red Horn return to their homes.
I mistake my flesh for meat
and eat it. In those days
the summer was kept in a bag
tied to the lodge-pole. Precious things.

Trickster why do you bleed
from the anus when you could have helped me split these logs.
Winter is almost on us, on our backs.
I am the last to know myself.
It is down to bone. My body

feels its ancestors stirring in anger, in
bewilderment. My children find in me
a mother with dried breasts. They
cry for my attention but
between a man and a woman there is so little to say

that has not been said
in better times. We must reform ourselves
against the contempt of things that knew our
touch once. I do not know
if I have the tools to do it.

Paracentric

"As one grows older one becomes
less clever and more personal…"
from the notebook.
                      There is this solidity of things

which vanishes. Or you see
only the bones
not the lovely body walking with its books
on the grass, under the high sun.

I wonder what my ancestors would make of me now
crowded into this space I have called
my self for too long
                      this sunlight

I feel I don't share
and am jealous of. The old

crazy connections fade
before some need to survive, to feel
the gravity of the long invisible line I have been
walking
                      which I perceive now

to have had its
fatal colors, misdirections, smells
I attached to those I loved
                      and thought my own.

To accept this change
is an exorcism
but not an answer.
Something primitive in you cannot plead
but must accept, like Oedipus
              exile and grove

to the turning of some moment when his hands
cease to be strangers who had done those things
and the bodies return, living, naked
with words of this world
                      foreshadowing another

and another
daughter who will live and bear your name
until her change comes
and the light returns
in ways you could not have invented.

The Text

One has been there and one has not. Two might have made it a place, an occasion, to remember. But two were not there: one had to invent the other, so the place and the occasion were fictitious, and what one saw truly with his eyes was his own falsehood, pleading with the wind, the waves, and the gulls to confirm his legend: as Odysseus' legend, lying open on his knees, was confirmed by the ocean, looking east, the early morning sun, at the place he had marked and left open, as if to attract what might come riding in on the waves of this more northern sea at the beginning of his day.

  He writes one word in the margin: Open. He waits.

Stillness moves one. Movement holds one still. It is from movement that legends are born. It is in stillness that legends are written. The two make an occasion and a place. What is one up to, thinking he is thinking, unnerved by stillness, unable to move, sitting here at a place where the sun touches the sea, nakedly, without mind: waiting for something to open, for another to appear and call his name.

  He closes the book on the word he had written, and waits.

One outwaits one's perfection. One waits and waits to be made incomplete. One is added to one, or one divides and grows: one becomes two, three, four, ten, and loses the godhood of the sun, and is everything under the sun, all things, all systems, all laws, but can never return: can never be that which never leaves itself and so never returns.

  He opens the book and writes three words in the margin:
  Monad, Nomad, No-man. He waits.

The primal fire, from which all things come, to which all things return. He lights a cigarette and draws a circle in the margin. He touches the tip of the cigarette to the circle, and the circle burns, expands. Its black edge eats the words he had written, eats into the text of the sun, the beginning of his day, and stops for no reason at the O of Odysseus, whose journey is not yet complete, and therefore not fully begun: as one must know the end before he begins: the stillness in the movement of the heart.

He tears out the burnt page and waits.

Mummy, what is that man doing burning all the pages of his book and throwing them into the sea?

FIGURE OF EIGHT

1987

Making Plans

*I worry too much about the sound
of wind*

*happen I sent those messages too late
to attract what scars need
reopening*

*a dog now, a dog
but in winter the temper can turn
dangerous*

*distance is precisely the will
it takes to cover it*

*but without masks how can we meet
and equal ourselves*

*in space above cloud cover
two shadows slipping past missing
each other's grip*

*tremblingly
intentionally
with such regret.*

For A.G., Both S.W.'s and A.M. the figure of morning

Figure of Eight

"Mientras la sombra pasa de un santo amor"

Antonio Machado, *Del Camino*

"…this essential nothingness of the imagined object…"

Jean-Paul Sartre

"It's one thing to love New York
It's another thing to live there
Baby I know you're lonely"

Sam Higgins, 'Baby I Know You're Lonely'

Premonition

She kicks off her jewelled sandals.
The rain will wash her feet.
The long hair of the rain
will hide her eyes. Any moment
the way is lost and must be looked for
without footsteps, the gaze
always the gaze, breaking
through heavy cloud. Wild animals
living the night through their eyes
as we live by fire, whisper
this is not the way. Turn east, turn west
plod north or glide to the south
it is all one where the spirit stands
barefooted in the rain
waiting. She gathers the young trees
and eats them leaf by leaf
drinking the rain. Blood collects
in the footprints she leaves behind.
On Broadway the lights flash out her name
a hundred years from now, the
wind that turns the rain-wheel
rises and dies, circling her feet.
She moves as a flute breathes
through all the stops and ghosts of air.
The lights flare in our bone-cells.
It rains as it never rained.

FIGURE OF EIGHT

"En la bendita soledad, tu sombra"
Antonio Machado, *Del Camino*

"That girl standing there"
W.B. Yeats

I

Frost a little like Yeats
a great poet no one wants to be
caught dead sounding like

and Pound might have got it wrong
but Lowell's excursions into history
were fruitless, mirrors just

to magnify the self
and diminish the anguish of time

What Pound suffered at last with the Jews
was incarceration and the threat of death
the wages of love, to survive this

but eventually the stories get told
yours, mine, in whispers or through
that silence which is terrifying

because it is "its own nothingness"
the gap in the journey that annihilates
the entire road. So far one goes

has gone, must come again
to where the pathway and the feet
are identical, and you are not

the figure lost or I the shadow left.

II

That afternoon
the rain came
riding the back of the wind
we watched, naked behind the screen
and couldn't make love, the wind and rain
did it for us, and you sang
a love song from your village
it moved in the wet air and rush
of water through leaves and grass
the trees shook their ankle bells
and flung their hands
"an unbroken continuity
of existence in itself"
to borrow words from Jean-Paul
who was as remote from that moment
as you are gone now
beyond the Manhattan skyline
city, city, the great divide
the "empty world of laughter" as you put it
to walk out in the lamplight
as the snow drifts down
a hundred years ago
an hour from now
"for the most beautiful girl in the world
can offer only what she has"
that circle of light in the dust
which Lakshman drew around Sita
to protect her from her story
the imperative of her own fate
the passion of rain falling
bent-headed into open hands

but she went back under the earth
and Rama grew tired of life
and crept to the river's edge
and vanished as a fish slips through its ring.

III

While I was making coffee
this morning in October
a coral snake climbed up a dead ivy vine
to the window sill, its tongue alert
for early autumn insects

pretty the quick black eyes
I checked for holes in the screen
the fissures in my own skin
and watched it swing slowly from vine to vine
in a pattern remembered from dreams

repeating the dance figure
anchored at head or tail
of your feet on the boards of the stage
the lock and pivot somewhere in
the lifeline of the body

at points that varied, as a poet will
his rhythms, or a dancer's breath
then loosing its grip to fall
flat to the ground, its whole length
never the head first

a moment to recover
then the slow crawl, this cobra relative
through the skelter of ants at the wall's foot
like Pound in the tent at Pisa
to learn it all again

from memory to climb the sunlight
genius of beginnings with no ends, life
forever ahead of the sentence one reads
or creates, as
your body in repose, your body

wanting our eyes wants more
breaking and saving the figure, the double
circle of time returning on itself
both snake and dancer
patterning as did Yeats, or Frost the native

or as Lowell wanted, something too close
two bodies at bed in the heart
the earth-smell stronger than either
the beauty of nature in no way
comparable to that of art, which is its own end

(to paraphrase) and yours
pretty one, the kiss
between us this distance now
and "What is this separation?" you ask
the sunlight and October air

this nothing and all ... Insect words
flit at the tip of my tongue, the dead
vine my lifeline even as I crawl
hungry into winter. Love
I eat my words, am filled with emptiness.

IV

They brought him hemlock and he
drank it like a snake
his dancer's mind accepted
the body was old and should go

and form was everything
form, the pattern, the artistry as it
touched on things and gave them shape
shape to live by, shape to die

the thread through which the spirit moves
that breaks and remains the same
in the anguish of knowing
nothing lives up to itself

or can ever return

An old man falls into silence
having said everything
and finally "I was wrong, I was
mistaken"

but nothing can change that now
the enormous tragedy of the dream
is the form the body is left with
the pattern it leaves
                is silence

and every voice that ever spoke
the sadness of your eyes in repose
the dark light of laughter there

after love and rain.

V

Do cries fall
in the category of silence
      the thought itself is enough
hidden away in a blood-cell
or a stone cell underground

how the body survives
what it knows is not the favorable air
of successful laughter, irony
of ironies, *iron maiden*

Osip Mandelstam
whose muse turned to hunger
in deep winter
      the cry the silence
edging into daylight like a spider
when the light fades

the one circled by nothing
the eye ringed by her admirers
the bride, her bachelors even
soledad

to live life to the hilt is such a
strange expression and must relate to
battle or murder, how
      else to draw the bull
onto your sword
who love that kind of dance
necesidad

which way do we go, what is the *tao*
who haven't phoned or will not phone
so long or write a simple note
or send it

if we are nothing and must create ourselves
as the wind creates deserts, trees
and gardens, excuse enough
               the tuft of inky hair
    soft where my fingers enter, make
the rain-dance

is memory
bitten tongues and words lost
in the wet silk of open mouths
commingling, dry by morning

how to be clear without confusing
issues which are forever confused
by definition, so
               wild the silence, its cries
of ecstasy, its unbound hair
the poet searching his garbage heap
sweating and freezing

"that beauty may be
in small, dry things"
an antidote to all this dampness
like a laundry line
               the Indian cotton print
torn beyond wear
washed and kept as a keepsake
vanidad

What gathers here
has no way out.
I open my hand and release
the invisible thing with wings.
I release you, your shadow is heavy.
The *mudras* change, your hands make
'a woman becoming two birds'.
You are out there now somewhere.

VI

My mother goes out one door
My father the other

the stage is empty, the theater
is full of invisible eyes
nothing moves

tungsten bears the silence
the light, well past the melting point
of human nerves

tension, at the point where lovers
break and separate
and the children continue to wait

watching that last place
where the two cast their last shadow
the invisible door that opened once and

closed ... The way you look for
is not the way. We are free to choose
what is visible, visibly ours

the thing in hand, the captive.
When the sun falls in just such a way
on that yellow stucco wall

something that flies away and hides itself
and later calls long distance
teases you with yourself. Your

being, your not being there
is the closest to touch I can come.

VII

Ill fate and abundant wine.
—Ezra Pound

The lives of fragments. This pathetic duty
to pick things up and put them back
where they belong. To tidy
the edges of life
so the center is clear, the circle where
you alone stand witness
to an orderliness which is forever
breaking and scattering in its own helplessness
what you love and protect with your life
or things simply gathered, how
to tell them apart, your
self from each one.
                    Dumb things without mouths
that shine in their quiet pleading to be kept
a little longer.
                I sent the box by freight
five working days to the tenth floor
New York address. The pink towel, the small
tape recorder, a *Norton Anthology*
some school notes and ballpoint pens, the old
leather sandals ... miscellaneous things
from the past now coming to crowd you.
I kept the little copper bell
that fell off the anklet, I keep
too much to myself, I take, misplace
things where they are not. They dance
a silent pattern on the carpet in the shadowy house
singing under their breath
so only the blood can hear it. As
my father would whisper her name

while he went about his carpentry
or stood at the sink rinsing things
over and over until we took them from him.
Summer too long where is fall the keen
Canadian wind
the clear streambeds of eyes, the
lassitude of honey.
                      Means and ends
"The honey of peace in old poems"
the clear viscosity clouded by the cold
of living fragments.
                      Why should the agèd
men, old men
should be
beautiful manners
                      a life for a life
for a time, picked apart like Penelope's threads
so the figure can return whole
in the mirror of the silent telephone
the unforgettable voice
at some number listed somewhere in the sky
of its lights at night
                      The box is sent
filled with oddments … a photograph
someone took of you in bed
who loved you but never touched you
as these words attempt to keep that touch
the wind knows and is expert at,
no human.

VIII

Not enough to speak the language of one's time
there is no such thing. Or to love
the lovers of one's days and nights
who are ghosts of others, who mourn
for you and for themselves.
                The name of this one I speak
over and over in the air she left
behind her. Name me, name me too.

The peripeteia, the journey never over nor
long enough. On a rock at a point where the path
turns, she is sitting, her face averted
waiting, waiting for something…
mas Ella no faltará a la cita, the
loss of others to others, or
to the expert wind. The merest change of light.

Matsya, the fish, the first
to come, the first
to return, among
the incarnations if
the circle holds.
            To know
the dancer from the dance, her hands
that make the shape of Krishna's flute
or fingering more intimate things in the ever
questioning never ending
city night, the bee
enters the flower, the flower
opens, and closes.
                Name me, name me then.

Brahmins not eating fish or flesh
for they are the forms of creatures that God
has taken in time, though man
eats woman, woman man
and the tree spreads its shadow over all
the north wind brings cold rain
the cigarettes are empty
                        Name me then

as another. Its own nothingness
returns as a figure of speech, a
paper or bamboo bird hung from the curtain rod
in the window facing east, a tender
photo of a *geisha* with a paper fan
too young to know much
                        someone's child
about to become
another's girl. Name her for me now.

No more elegies, *no más.*
So far one goes the long way home and on.
The light has hands and turns itself
so slowly from frown to smile
the day latening towards the coast
in sunlight on a clear road with the tape-deck playing
the light back to you
                        the evening *raga* sung
in the raw voice of the sea
the three descending notes repeating
                      naming you again
asking you to return. And you are gone.

En la bendita soledad, tu sombra.
In the blessed solitude, your shadow also.

A Perfect Stranger

Interstice

Deep as it appears to have gone
the way lies deeper

depth of rivers, depth of eyes
depth of hidden intentions

the hazy wind, the *amargo*
sea wind flutters in the tv aerials
above the village

some things move slightly
and others soar, it is all one body
a scarab, a mountain swift

the goats are coming down the mountain
leaping and jumping over the rocks
the thorny bushes

somewhere not in sight
a car is burning by the side of a road

nothing is there to watch it but these words

Patterns Leaves Make

The adams and eves are in the gallery.
In separate rooms the light changes
differently, my
remorse, a clock
running down.

In sugar maple weather
hands taste sweeter.
I dream I believe. A dusky skin
glows between buildings, moves
just out of reach. Your breath

is the silence it takes to speak
what is listened for
but might change. As a painting
turns from you and re-enters
the landscape it came from

or that face
already moving away
to ask its question somewhere else.

Of the light in the park.
Of one particular tree.
A perfect stranger.

Why Distance Is Necessary

Like the shuffling of feet under a table
where the cards lie in pairs, waiting to be played.
That one's friends were never quite sane.

The only monument is this earth.
The rest to charity, to those
who need something to hang on to.
Begin loving someone, the sound of wind

rising. Humor the refusal to eat breakfast
of the ones who are austere, and need to go places
where the thorns pick at their clothes
and sunrise is a stark command. But

touch what's soft, with the tenderness
of one who has fingers. Do not eat today
but eat tomorrow. The cry is not in your ears.

Minima

Out of our helplessness to live
one creates a world, a language, an order
or a disorder. Another dies.

The sum of atomic particles in a fig tree
is a terrifying vision. You are unhappy today.
You coil the world around your wrist and lie there
dreaming. The little owl of the heart

flies on soft wings. You are remembering words
seen up close; the finality of details held until they
tremble, the necessary kill. But the figs

are dry; they hang like shrunken
scrota at the tips of the fig trees,
abandoned children of a remote powerful father,
figments of mind-energy lost to the sun.

To correct our sense of loss we talk to people,
as you will tonight. Their words are the certain transcriptions
of what you're seeking, written in air, with fatal urgency.

Inhabitant

To tell a story find
its skeleton at the risk
of becoming it, you

wonder why the moth's wings
have lost their body
and hang waiting to fly

only if the web tears
the wind tears it. In this
infirmity of the light

something is shaping, a name
you might have been given
and be living with now

as someone you think you remember
in a room whose doors
all open inward

open before you touch them
crying, someone
enter or keep out, why

is my blood heavy
heavier than the light
heavier than the air I must breathe.

Chinese White

When Trickster put on
a deer's vulva and lay with
the chief's son, he too
bore children. The well

now filled with bones
is dry, and empty of tears.
The tears are in the bones.

When they are born
there is still time for
seasons. Late summer becomes
a winter's child, and the ones born

in autumn come to life
in the spring. At two
the eldest one said
"Sometimes at night

when my eyes are open
my eyes make dirt move
to a silly place". My friend

who might have danced
for fame and money
is finding life difficult, and
there are no swans in Austin

no pools of carp
reflecting the human beginner.
In early winter, rain
is the pattern. Rain on grey grass.

Save your girl children.
They will suffer
and bring great pain
before the sun goes down.

Primitive

In the singles bar
the Shulamite sings
her griefs, her wandering song
under the drugged artificial stars
that guide us home.

Never gave you enough credit for being
ordinary, the obvious, what we
live for. Not
the mountains, the long upland pastures
of sunlight and cloud. Heroes

above and below
the norms of love and being.
Awake in each other's arms we embrace
the emptiness elsewhere that keeps us
here where the journey began.

In the brain things go wrong.
What calls has fingers.
The bird just after dawn crying
scarlet, scarlet
in a nearby tree.

We have what we're not while it lasts.
A kitten born from an egg
with a snake's head, four human feet
curled together for warmth
before this first last sunrise.

Proof of How It Should Look

We asked for proof
of how it should look.
Our hands were full of shadows.

Something in the grass made us turn
to listen, and at sunset we stood
wanting proof there was
something there. The wind blew your hair

back, like strips of dry cedar,
sun-fragrant, and the grass
was listening for us to move.

I had a time in mind and you
another time; this looking west at the air
hurrying to reach us, the
shadow climbing our bodies

as if to see beyond us, farther than
why our hands weren't touching,
that we stood so still.

It is nearly October.
We have been here thirteen years.
Something moved in the grass
and didn't move us to move,

to turn, to listen. We are
eyeless like the trees now and
as sensitive to change, the rain

darkens our skin, the wind dries us.
How could we help but ask
for proof of what it might become, this
tension that cries in us to be.

The Gift

The gift of white roses
at coffee time, on the day the province
voted. White roses, pomegranates, tomatoes
and coffee, the red sweet cells
scraped out with a spoon. Sun in full haze
and bougainvillea as red
spilling over the white walls, our blood
sharpened from nightmare to words
in a single remark. That steep ascent through thorns
when night fell on us in the mountains
us and the children. And
José taking Ana on his back
up a climb a goat would have found difficult
coughing his lungs out at the top
but triumphant. And the gift of white roses,
roses, wet, sweet, against the bitter coffee,
the heart of it, the effort of a man, of friends.
"We cannot help but be
constantly surprised by these people,"
as Wittgenstein remarked about those who dissemble.
We are cautious about giving.
We must know what the gift means, that
whoever receives the gift must know its meaning.
Here the sun gives everything
and whoever chooses the sun's gift to give
to another, is godlike, and supremely intelligent.

Spain and Kafka

I

How exactly the paler shadows of the
black iron railings angle away
from the source of light, the white
house-fronts deepening as the
sun climbs. Their lines
straight or bent depend upon the surface
they cross. You watch, no two are alike.
But in memory they lose this, they
revert to the perfect symmetry of remembered forms
and faces, the
geometry necessary for patterns to survive
and be remembered. I think I could
draw that house in detail, remembering it,
but not your face, so wide across
the cheekbones and eyes, the way your
hair falls. And the outline of those mountains
so clear as I look at it now, would be
impossible. No
concept or abstraction
would capture that shape of time, its flow-lines
too much like memory itself to be remembered.

II

Formal demands, clear cries for help
from the senses –
dark falls in the room
where one cricket sings
invisible but everywhere
turning the black air into
white sound. He dreams of Felice,
not herself but the details she
reminds him of, his
memory's icon, worshipped like the nerves
he's cursed with. To know
everything, to be in touch without ever
touching, to stay beyond reach and
feel, hair by hair
her head forming in his hands, her
face her eyes but
incalculably distant, as if she has
died already and he
loves her for this, the details
too real even to be true. But her life
plain and solid, evades him
who feels the wind in his bones
the mole's terror in a human kiss.
"Someone must watch, it is said.
Someone must be there."

Soleá

Grey squirrel
sits on a
tree limb, its
tail tucked over it
like a tent
under the rain

the eyes of a wild animal
can never close, the
future watches there
remembering itself as an eternity
of questions the light asks
the sound of a pencil dropping

in the leaves, the
infinite activity of
lying in wait, a guerilla
in Nicaragua
or a grey squirrel framed
in a window of square panes
one's life, one's life

the autumn rain
that ages what it touches
fur and silence, fur
beyond blood-heat the cold
of stroking air
the mission, always the mission
beyond one's life one's means

green leaf, pale rain
grey features of the wind
and in between, the peace where
the thing itself lies still
withholds its life

at the target's very eye
where the self runs
in widening circles of asking
as if in some other life
these too would be its lives

the eye light
as a fallen pigeon feather
detached, patient, beyond desire
the green leaf nicked at the edge
by something that passed
too quickly to make sense

eye of the rain
heart-murmur, belly-whisper
precious skin, precise
surface of depth, touch
this, do not be afraid
your acids will erase it or
it turn to feed on you.

Multiples

Seed to architect
whoever made you
me to live in you

wants in wants out
the inner staircase
hidden, the
dark stairwell

as light is pressure
is air, the wind
inside moaning
through tall shafts through
tunnels, empty

apartments where the old seed
died or never came
the animate passageways
and stripped beds, single
where only mirrors

a black curled hair
on the toilet edge, foot
print lost in carpet, dry
air from the shower head
some one, am I

too late, breasts
the hungry milk trapped
in hollow metal handrails
down as up
the seed runs out

rain on window
wind inside the rain
effortless, effortless
the terror to be free

or fucks the air
the lost egg dreaming of
multiplying, logic
of ambivalence, love
its language *ecce*

ecce homo a woman
making her own wind, her
mind up in the sound of his voice
as she answers, what

language is ever shared, what
skin to skin passion of
smoke loitering
in fireproof corridors

the seed rains
the egg is breaking
glass shatters as
someone is running has
left this hole for our words.

And Language Is Everything

This philosopher I knew, his
baby sat in its highchair
and was attracted to the flame of the match
he'd struck to light his pipe.
He gave it the match to hold and it screamed.
"I love that child," he said.
"I want it to learn the difference between
appearance and reality, brilliance and fire."

We left the house and watched the cool stars forming
familiar patterns, as our eyes adjusted.
I thought he was right, and that the baby should kill him.

Andalusian Spring

A battle formation of heavy women in black
moves arm in arm up the street
formidably lost
in life's shadows. No wind

shall pass between them. Old and young
founder as one wave upon the
only possible shore. The sun-filled
yellow spring flowers

struggle past
like girlhood, unnoticed.
When someone dies one is kind.
For the living there is patience and a swept house.

The Village

He kept on seeing her as the grapes
ripened and the wild goats
came down and ate them. Being
but not being-there, his triumph

in time as empty as the sunlight that
was always there, and her ankles
always dusty and cut by the sharp grass
at the edge of the path. So our bodies

wandered, the backs were all we saw of each other
for days. Eyes for the world, for other eyes
that were the world. Time, nerve

and the money it takes
to buy back your lucky star
more than a pocket can hold.

Assia

If I am to stay where you put me
give this note to the one who was expecting me
a white ribbon tied in her hair
unravelling now. In the doorway of that

shop that is about to close
how to tell the difference, but for the eyes
concealing the knowledge of a lost property
as a light that is fading. Who

of her own dark generation having escaped
to live this long, who, of her wandering kind
solo now, the stage hers, weeps silently.

The woman who waits becomes
less and less visible. When night falls
she is the whole of darkness waiting to go.

Climbing

I noticed in the mountains this time, seven years later
a configuration of myself and you
as memories of each other, the one
ahead, the other behind, climbing
in the same place. It didn't seem right to be here,
to have repeated this
time and place so strong and the same figures
retarded by this: the
man and the three children, and the fourth
who was not born then: reliving for ourselves, our
selves the fact of our repeating this, as if
too deliberately, as proof we were not wrong
about something we knew by heart, only
ourselves? The old trails, sharp with stones
peppered with goat droppings
didn't know what we were asking. And there was
a reluctance to use the camera, a
desire to get beyond range of what was
obvious, while yet repeating
the obvious, as we have always done, and the children too
by habit. But this place was too important.
It had fed us too long with a vision of what we might
really become, not for the
asking, but for the
taking. These mountains beyond range of our home
above valleys of tragic olives, suffering for rain,
too strong to be held close: the fine line
between wanting and having, memory and repetition.
I make too much of this. But without this question
it is all a painting of solid primary colors
arranged in patterns a child could grasp

as a child climbs, easily. Or as our life has been
the effort of unravelling fear, without breaking it,
so as to be attentive to rain as it falls
and feel at our roots the air the rain won't open.

Homecoming

Something like a skateboard, and
the Toronto skyline. See how fast I can go
before time thickens the cement at my wheels
and everything stops. Then

it is vertical. The face
beneath a city gazing up
like the drowned French airman still wrapped
in his parachute lying
on gently sloping sand. Not

the dead, but in the eyes
a kind of perpetual last words
in a new language. The poem
waiting to break from the mind

as Dutch Schultz lay dying
in Newark City Hospital
in late October under a clean moon

"The sidewalk was in trouble
and the bears were in trouble and
I broke it up ... Please mother
you pick me up now. Please
you know me"

Or as in the city where you came from
there is a corner where the air feels familiar
and we have not met yet, the spice
or is it the scent you wear
lingers. And no name is mentioned ever.

Black Glass

The reddish grey iron
afterglow of sunset, between
shadow and space. The numbers of eyes.
She says "I'm growing old," and November
echoes the sounds,
a house without pictures or heat
to which strangers come as possessors
staying late and talking too loud.

This loneliness beyond intimacy. Our
chosen exile. What the sun sends down
breaks into details like a china cup –
the shock of separation, the
suddenness beyond words of what we try to capture
as ourselves. To love poetry is to be
always a beginner. Too much leaks through
one knew was important, and

it becomes a game of ageing, always
a sunset, the effervescence of all
colors in that one ruby fire
too close to the blood. These signs cry for attention
sometimes. If it were not so
would we be making love so deep in the night
while only half awake,
in the blackest hour when words fail us like eyes.

Full Moon Story

"¿Eres la sed o el agua en mi camino?
Dime, virgen esquiva y compañera."

Antonio Machado, *Del Camino*

I

Mother, cradling the sky
in your loose blue sleeves
wind arrows the yellow wheat
forever, it seems, in one direction
and I walk behind you

You never turned
to ask me who I am
I am unidentified still
a man without identity, a
father without speech, words, for his daughters

And the water continues to flow
Kitaro, under Fujiyama
the owl, the tuk-too, flute-calls
peace, love, the innocence that is evil
the evil that is tolerable

because it is lovely.
I am free to write
my question-mark in your womb
curled, the foetus, as my hand lies
curled against your thigh

hoping for a second birth
the touch that failed, the touch that
flashed between us in late May
two people alone, each wanting
the lost half of the world in the other's body

Chords of electronic wind
frenzy the bamboos by the mountain stream
the water's nipples rising

like raindrops, like small fish
nestlings cheeping for food

The music is over. The music is gone
with your song in the far distance
I think I can't reach. My clothes
smell of yesterday's bed
and today's carpets. The nerves

are steadier than they should be.
I am strong, strong
with the strength of the weak
who must stay still to survive
or of the very powerful

whose mere gestures can destroy.
I am the monster you gave birth to
so gladly. The one so full
of hunger even the stones
aren't safe. The music is over

and the wind returns
formless, inhuman. Give me back my name
to play with again. I
gather you in my arms. I gather
emptiness, as a dancer gathers eyes.

II

The heart is a chord
that must be played with care
or it unhappens.
Words that don't burn are no good.

Truth seeks itself.
The melting and freezing sensation
between us, within us
leaves no room for comfort, no room

where the door opens on perpetual sunlight
or on twilight, the hour you're most
afraid of. In your hands
I am all things I have been

but the future resembles a bone
someone tossed in the grass
after a feast. I love you in your
freedom, but

as another woman said
"The absolute freedom of the human creature
is horrible." And beautiful too
in the pattern you make of it

the ever-open question. At Easter
the children insist on their candy
chocolate eggs and rabbits
beyond the age for such things. They were

mine to play with, now they play with me
as you play, the chord in me
that sings and burns. Over the hills
the whole city lies with you

in a deep sleep. It is too early to live.
Self, I whisper, self
how do I gather these fragments?
Her skin was always softer than my hand.

III

At fifty a man should settle for less
than the whole
but that thing always burns
"The devil" he said, pointing to his crotch
what changes is what's happened
and the spaces between, the missing parts
can only resemble what's happened
though it is late the world is young

We talk all night and
go to bed in the cold
too tired to do it
The voice that sings in your dream reaches me
as whales communicate
in the elemental telepathy of the ocean

which is where we swim
seeking each other

Though by daylight the music has changed
syncopated with the clock
that watches us
              the hundred streams
shed by the sacred mountain
announce Manhattan and the perfume of
studios mad to get the least note right
before the light burns out

As in my nerves
the coffee spills
and leaves a bloodstain on the floor
your dress immaculate white
your eyes so dark there's no telling it is day

This is love then
This is the body's time between
askings of touch, the bee
hovering above the half-open flower
myths of whatever gods, who never grow
old or tired
               what bird is that
you ask
calling in the valley, but

I must go
I must go, it is getting late
The truth is I have stayed too long
The truth is the truth, I
lose myself in you

I am angry for my lost self
I am angry with you

IV

I touch your body in an animal's eyes
your hunger, your wariness
of this old encroachment, this

almost-trap of a different
harmless nearness. How can I erase

my shadow from the earth, live
as pure light, a thought
your hand needn't touch? My smell

circles me always, like holy fire.
Your smell belongs with the night

it breathes, it eats, it leaves no shadow behind.

V

Mother or placenta-twin
lost at birth
whatever the verdict now.

I have grown old beyond the power of my hands
to bless or touch your body
as a lover would. Not true

not true. But yes
I think of you
this meaningless Easter, under a clouded sky

and a south wind. You dance for your own gods
create, preserve, destroy
your breath is their life

your gift. But where am I
this swirl of wind, this
snail-shell filled with dust

which is life's
abundant pattern? Man to man
the mirror I become in time

cracks and shatters. The world seen through glass
only resembles the world, we
cut so easily. A woman is old

is everything, and is always in her youth.
Your blue sleeves trail the sky across the earth
in the manner of wind, and I breathe

in joy, in anger. Today the Japanese wind
moves me as the colors blue and yellow.
The Indian wind in your eyes

darkens this. Somewhere at the heart of it all
someone suffers, writhes, hangs limp
and comes to life in a dream

I can't imagine. It is the son
you will never have, the
god or lover your will asks for

never to be born, of you or anyone.

The animal that prowls in all our hearts
has no shape or name, but the silence of old wounds.

VI

The full moon speaks
a dead language
one round vowel
then silence

For nine months we've shared our grief
I want your happiness, the
seed the moon denies
she stares too long and hard
her synthesis can drive men mad

and make a woman selfish
a will too pure, as Yeats thought
to belong in the world.
The bamboo clacks and rustles in the wind
both grass and instrument

a perfect fit in the hand
a dancer who loves crowds, and with
one of the stubbornest roots, wandering
God knows where, under the hard moon.

Kitaro, solitary of the mountain water
or Antonio Machado who lost her
when she was very young
and wandered his own river, talking to trees

full moon, full moon, my dancer
to release the animal in you and keep
also the pure intention

beggars that these words are

supplicants at the mother's torn hem.

CHILD EATING SNOW

1994

for Guit, and the road to Campillos

Baby Upside Down in a Light Snowfall

The ones we know and recognize
through the flame, they smile and are gone
before we can name them   As memory is
what otherwise we would forget
what cries for forgiveness.
The mouths   the tiny mouths of snow that burn us.
The white nails of our mothers playing us wildly angrily.

Blue Fur Hood

Here are my eyes. Almost all the mirrors
are gone from the house, what I see
wherever I look, is myself
multiplied, in all possible forms.

So, in the light snow falling, I think of you
and reach for the telephone, your voice
furred with air of unbroken animal time
inside the wind. My brother's death

meant winter all over again, the dark eyes there
this time, like holes in the snow, cooing of Inca doves
lost in white smoke. *Being dead is*

hard work I remember from one of the Duino
Elegies. And also, *Every angel is terrifying*
in your breath's voice, white across thin blue air.

Christopher

I know what it cost him to be born
In the likeness of a younger brother
walking behind us, aware
of the backs and backs of heads
and running feet going past him
and the dark humorous forgiving eyes
waiting for someone to turn
and wait for him to follow
because he never chose to walk ahead
though his legs were longer than ours
his head inches taller, his brain
at least as good. When our mother died
young, of cancer, he was too green
he was not prepared for her memory.
In every shadow there is still
a picture of her face:
and the shadows he saw as he, young
lay dying of cancer last March
must have been too frightening
for him to ask me to name them.
Our love lay not with language
but with silence. There is a speech
the grass breathes for us. It is summer
and the wind coming off the hills of the Gatineau
is filled not with sorrow but with time.

Fugitives

The old woman said
*If you know where home is
you know everything.* But the
grindstones in her yard
whispered
"You, you tormented us.
Every day, every day
at night, at dawn
all the time our faces went
holi, holi,   huqui, huqui
because
your children were hungry."

I would prefer an apartment
furnished in white, she said.
This is the song of home. These
are the words that enter my
house. My son and daughter
live here with me.
Spirit of disorder
Enemy of boundaries
Trickster, let go. Let go.

Their eyes were wide open at night
They ate raw meat raw vegetables
When frightened they attacked
with nails and teeth. It said
He walks *as if he is in a shadow*
And she does nothing *thinking, thinking
sitting by herself
and thinking her own life.*

Madame Matisse, 'The Green Line', 1905

How can we bear to be separate
the shadows ask the light, the light
the shadows. On both sides
of the green vertical line
running from hairline to chin
her full dark eyes gaze with such power
the paler, the darker face
is not divided by it.
Green of youth, green of death
his ambiguous gift to her, that she be
both at once, a woman of her time.

Migrations

Springtime teases us. In that
chunk of brown wind
a flock of sparrows
humped under the weight
of flight, dropped
scattered, pock
pock, to dust.

Out of Africa
the long long drift north to a paler skin.
Out of time and in time the shrill
ungathered music of the birds
watching, watching us. Against

the pure blue illusion of sea
a child, a dark child, plays in the waves.
Another, a bird, at rest, watches us.

It this had been a garden in my heart.
A man with a burnt hand
A woman with burnt fingers
asking directions *the nearest way to the light*
No face, no need of features
as the first faint flames begin
to drift on the wind

It is a city burning.

Child Eating Snow
For my niece Sylvia

In the wilderness she
imagined she grew up in
there was this photograph
of a child eating snow.
Handfuls of years
back behind memory now
and not her face at all
the eyes different
like a bird's eyes
eaten out by the wind.

II

In the winter sun that year
her father was all bone. Slowly
he was turning white
like her shadow on the snow.
In her dreams she never saw the sun
but sometimes a vivid suffusing light
like a torch shone through water
reminding her
of the first cry
of her birth.

III

On the tenth of March
a door opened somewhere along the horizon.
Her father left her. His dark eyes
return at night, beyond the stars
behind the snowflake.

The bird cries again
Cry I can't imitate
No eyes it has

IV

The blue static of lights along the freeway
grows colder, turns warmer
turns to flame. *Snow*
is how mirrors looked
before I was born the old woman remembers.
The sun squats in the grass
like a dam-bear. It is brown like her father's eyes.
Silent, as a mouth stopped with snow
her memory of this picture.

V

She sits in her mother's shadow.
She is eating the snow from his face.
Winter whispered her name, summer will
sing it now. The
single bird's cry
is a forest of music of leaves.
But it is still winter she said.
It is still February in my hands.

VI

The day is at breakfast.
Things, things to do.
Will the clouds leave the windowpane?
She's skating on last year's ice.
Wings hover above her, soft
hunter's wings. *Falcon, soul*

exiled among ravens, Father, your shadow.
It is summer.
The sky is mother blue
in the winter she imagines
she will live in forever.

VII

The child is eating the snow.
Her hunger is her thirst
her thirst her hunger. Her
father dies, her mother is alive.
Between seasons she draws breath
like a creature in hiding, to survive
what might watch her too long
too intently for love. So
she whispers her own name
Bird, how old am I
How old
is the rain in the summer grass
beyond mercy   beyond memory
Bring it to me. Bring it now.

Moving On, and with a Glance at Rilke

Hawks above the sheer drop
at Arcos de la Frontera
at eye level drift across
the wind at sunset. Or
off the edge of the *alameda* at Ronda
that winter of '13. The few
Spanish poems. The bust in the hotel garden.

What birds plunge through is not the intimate space
in which you see all forms intensified.
Nor in summer as I drive
the long switchback road up through the hills
where the shepherds whistle to the stones
to follow them home. *I am*
the cold wind. There is a time

the father must leave his daughters. Call them
poems then. A game
we used to play in the snow
making the shapes of wings in the snow.
In the brute heat of July
the angels fly as the dust. They're
like words without a language, no use to anyone.

I must leave you now because
you are too hurt, you hurt too much.
To go our separate ways. To enjoy
that most terrible drug – ourselves –
which we take in solitude as
Walter Benjamin said. The
absent ones, the ones who fall as rain

on our funerals and festivals, in our eyes
and when we're joking. At heart
a prophecy, always. The going, the separation
always. It takes such training, it is what
we breed ourselves for, groom our shy
mirrors to tell us. I resign. I resign.
I retire. Because of the time

it has taken me to grow halfway old
and autumn has become my nature, the
autumns of first encounters –
you, and you, and you – what are the
silks we should wear for our loves? Always the
last word. So it is with poetry.
The cry from what is left of the heart.

Exuberance (Paul Klee)

As I danced along the tightrope
I failed to see
the figure of a woman
in dark mourning blue
lurking in the lower
right-hand corner, watching
her back pressed
against a patch of red

the same red that surrounds
my face my beating hands
not the sky blue that encloses
the upside-down man falling
the exclamation mark at upper center

there are greens, there are other colors
at lower left a tiny dog
or deer, a straw star
high up, and a hand
above the woman's head
or is it a crown of fire
and the black scorch marks in opposite corners

teetering on my rope
I danced with all my hands
it was 1939
I failed to see the hidden
woman shawled in dark blue mourning
in one corner
I failed to see
dead center
the booted man in brown with huge shoulders
beginning to scream at me.

Separation in the Evening (Paul Klee, 1922)

Two arrows point
from earth to evening
evening to earth.

There is the ceremony where the two meet
and never meet, like our tongues
touching, or our tongues
speaking. One

descends from dark violet twilight.
The other rises from sunlight
in its earthiest desert colors.
Together they are everything
that begins invisibly and ends
invisibly. In the few inches between

the meeting of the arrows
I touch you now.
I try to touch you now.
It is where the space is neutral, neither
sky nor earth, and your
lips are open. It is the wind

we both imagined was our bodies.
It is the evening.

Couplets Late September

The geese are beginning to fly south
the snows and the canadas.

My twenty-first autumn in this house.
Their cries are the only sound

between the earth and the sun.
It is the cry with no home –

time is their wilderness.
Time is this house. My home

is a direction I haven't taken, where
memory is, waits

bien e tan mesurado
with dignity and restraint

for someone else to come
who is no one and needs nothing.

I envy that man, woman, child, thing
who is without identity

whose hands play with the wind, uttering cries
that echo off nothing human.

The Structure of the Ground

In Paul Klee's *God of the Northern Woods*
done in 1922 a face
looms out of a background of squares
and muted colors, yellow, purple, green
in the key of darkness
boreal, silent, closed.
The surface is scattered with crosses
like stitches.
I asked my way and was told
these were not your ancestors but ours.
You lie on the dry bed of pines
and deep moss of a far older dream
than is good for you. We
who made the earliest fires
that melted back the snow and ice
have no place for you in our circle.
The face that you see in the paint
draws us to a close as a book shuts –
unwillingly. And you can never forget it.

Paris, 1957

A Citroën Deux Chevaux
parked against the curb
on a rainswept boulevard
and passing this side of it, her
heel lifted, a hurrying woman
whose shadow falls towards me

is how the dead might see us
at play in a photograph
no colors in their world but
light and shadow, and very little light

(or lovers the old hotel
whose name they've forgotten
the street, the exact address lost
off the edge of memory)

anonymous and lovely
the car in the rain, the shadows
the woman hurrying along the wet street
are all the mother we have
who watches us, late as it is.

Then

At the turn of the century
a dog trotting across an intersection
pauses to reflect on the sunset.
There, his ghost receives him
and whatever angels are left to feed upon
howl at the center of his eye
for the juxtaposition of sun and moon
the old lovers, to bear him on
over the snow fields of everywhere else
his puppy wit, his delicate silence now.
In the cave where they bore him, his parent shadows
toss dice to determine the course of the sun.
Now he is a long way from home.
Nothing comes with wings to soften him.

Poem Depending on Dashes

But here with winter about to begin
a cold whisper in the leaves
and the woods full of ghostly deer
hidden between cracks of sunlight, where
looking I see only my old self
in a still place, a posture of waiting
the gun, the loving fingers of
those old vanished habits we shared
one autumn, or was it ten –
before something or someone called you
but – and the words that come now
Love is to me that you
are the knife which I turn
within myself – are Kafka's
by accident I recall, more than chance
which is a touch different if only
less violent – here
in this house farthest from your life
but which I imagine I love
as I can imagine we loved
despite all that happened, death, death
and your death –
the leaves ask no questions, or the grass
lacking the thousand human mouths
that are born to cry and devour
what we are, what we were – But
I am what remains of the eyes we shared
the noises, winds, voices, smells
as if it were a single animal
haunting itself – the shed trees, the
stamped lights of houses along the road
back, always back to this – the leaves –
the sentence never finished

Jeanne d'Arc

The wind that licked her hair
we touch in our secret places, the flames
like kittens at her fingers. Who knows
from what direction it blew that day. The sun
squeezed in her fierce hand was mute, diminished.
But it took a good while for her heart to open,
the wine dark door. And they drank
all day and night in the taverns, spelling her
name wrong as they shouted it: oaths, jokes, smut
where the artist's pencil shaded her body
and moved on into the cooler light of dawn.
What harm lingers in the smoke above the ash pile.
Where are we, you and I, among all these faces
that died by fire? And lost their names in hers?

Jeanne d'Arc (2)

At this intimate point, here where the
skin retreats, asking to be
put back, asking not to be brought out of
hiding, hurt, aroused, caressed, talked to
in whispers: here, say, here
is the *soul* at that moment, the wanderer,
he or she who lives from light to shadow. And
is the light in shadow. So if you'd asked the fire
why it began to sing, after the crescendo of
her cries had faded, it might have said
The life I stole from her. The voice of grief
singing of the air that had gone forever.
So the little square closed around her ashes
like a lost page in this book I close tonight.

Jeanne d'Arc (3)

October, the light moves once again
around the wheel of colors, turns inward, the reds
and browns beginning to ash out. Our bodies are
more delicate now in the morning cold.
I see her wandering among the trees, a
paradox of incommutable light
in the forest above the house. Her fingers trail the wind
through spider hangings where little leaves get caught.
This is our autumn, our shared time,
the live and the dead fire. My skin
burns when you take my hand and won't let go.
There will come a morning when everything seems clear
I imagine: when the clenched hand of fire opens
and releases you. And we can breathe again.

Ethnic Poem

Should the town fall before we get there
before the ripe red apples fall,
in the neighbourhoods some of you remember
the shadows begin to fret among themselves
and the roofs burst to let in the whole sun
like a game we once played as children
of changing the world while we slept,
and in the morning, not winter, not spring
but this white ash from which we rise again,
whole families come together
who had died during the night, and now
meet at the foot of the broken stair
to kiss and sing the old songs
we know by heart – the melody, not the words.

Namelessness

By now after all these years
I don't know who the "you" is any more
when the word writes itself instead of a name
or an honest detail. I had forbidden myself
this vagueness, this evasiveness
which is like the shadow that follows this pen
across the page. I had said
honor her memory, or hers, or hers
or speak of the subtle dark one I am with
who asks, what am I to you, am I
nothing? I have fallen into this habit
of remembering what comes easy to the heart.
You have no name. There is no smell in you
of skin or hair. Your body's word is gone.

Old Legends

Where the wind goes it breathes
sometimes such damaging testimony
that I am at a loss to know
who sent you here. You were one
to whom I said I love you
not enough, or was it too often
for both of us. I sleep badly at nights
imagining how poorly we both lived
what was given to us, a kind of beauty
that need not have depended on others
who said they loved us. We did, we do
ourselves such fatal injury. Now
I confuse you with what I remember of you.
We are such shadows. Yours is more alive.

A Thought from Yeats

I have had sex up to here
he said, indicating his chin
and now I want my life to be
my own, to be worth something more
than just a prick and a cunt
touching like utter strangers at an airport
lined up to board their flight. Why
the hell can't we ever get it straight.
Life, I mean. By which I mean
what we are really here for, not
what I am to her or she is to me.
It takes you so long to grow up
and then you grow old. Then all you do
is scream for it like a baby left all night.

Annunciation

When the messenger comes, it
might be just the postman
or it could be a face so filled
with joy grief or plain indifference
you are tempted to say, I know you
what is your message, what
thing can you tell me. Then
if the news is bad
you have your whole past to lean on
give you strength. But if it is good
what gravity will permit you to bear
the ecstasy, the unexpected
flight of shining wings that lift you
high above the bent head hung in prayer.

Where the Soul Goes in Summer

At night I jumped up
and brushed the spider off me
I had been having a dream
to which there came a spider

There was a spider
it was missing one leg
it was crawling away across the floor
I took my shoe and finished it

When I slept again
ten fingers stept across the wall
two eyes lay hid in thin cracks watching.

Love Poem

If the light were greener now
what monkey would come lost
to share in this meeting of lips
an apple could tell
a pomegranate bob roll fall
in the wake of islands
then whose mouth will drink this
I ask you she said.

Things That Can't Speak

While the national rifle association
feeds off the dead, I wonder what
their children eat. There are
reptiles that lie in wait
in holes or among stones
listening. A lizard I found once
in the sierra above Mante by a creek
a big lizard blinking at me slowly
from the shadow of a rock. I saw
that its claws were dug hard in the dirt.
Then suddenly it jerked back
as if pulled from behind
and I noticed that a long snake
had caught it by one leg
and was dragging it back, back
with infinitely slow irresistible pressure
to its lair under the rock
where its taut body lay coiled.
I watched it for almost an hour
a battle so utterly silent
you felt no fear or pain.
From time to time the lizard would gain an inch
but the snake took it back.
As the lizard regressed
towards death beneath that rock
for the snake it was progress
a contest so slow, so elemental and old
that for me to watch it was like
an unseemly intrusion of the future
an eye too quick to be there.
I did not see the end.
But I have tried to imagine it.

To recall in our time of sudden death
the tenacity of a far older will
its need to feed and survive
that long moment when a life cries no.

Ethnic Poem II

A baby hung in the wind
from an apple tree. The hills beyond
seemed high and endless, there were
patches of snow on the fields
or limestone showing through the grass.
Though the picture told me no date
I had come here before, whether by foot
or by horse and in whose company
I couldn't remember. And this time
the baby seemed more personal, a
thing I had been sent here to account for
to imagine its name, its father's eyes
and mother's hands. They had said
you will come to this mountainous land
and find there what you came to find
far from your own life and touch it
and give it your name. Is it
a girl or a boy I asked the lingering wind
for nothing else moved. Then let her
remember I came. Let her hear at least
my footsteps on the loose stones
as I walk away and do not look back.

A Man I Once Knew

There were afternoons the dark came suddenly.
The mountain grew quiet, the olive trees
took back their shadows. Then in the old light
you felt the first pressure of rain
as a faint thickening in the blood
a tensing of roots under the field stones
before the storm broke. And if
the storm cloud passed and no rain came
the old light would linger for days like a memory
of something other than meaning, more austere
than self discovery or happiness or grief.
That is the beauty of old villages, he said.
They have been there so long they become
the weather, the light. And we can only watch.

Andalucía

The Long Semesters

Autumn,
the trees are filled
with leaves of absence.

Spring Break –
and after that
the broken spring.

From a Painting by Munch

Winter, traces of wind
flickered about the streets
peppered our eyes. Impossible to tell
what was bothering her, like the girl
in Edvard Munch's *Ashes*
who stares and stares
from a well deeper than grief.

The memory of some healer forever alive
or the dream of it beyond
the pine trunks behind the darkened lake.
And her long dry auburn hair
stroking his shoulder there where he broods
huge, dressed in black, the eyes hidden

is at the edge of a scream
hers, their silence.
We felt the need to talk
which always betrayed us. Though because
of the cry of loneliness beneath our words
and as the season was summer, not winter
it was a risk neither of us wanted.

Obedience to the glory of the morning sun
and the last cold turning now to spring
returning, I should say
to catch both the habit and wonder of it
nothing for it but to remain still
to capture both the habit and the wonder.
In her heart

a song flies off every second and is
rarely heard. Therapies
curl, twist and circle her tears
which well up in the hard glaze of noon
or the deep blue of memory. The girl
is lost and the woman can't
find her. Her torn white dress

is more than the night can hide
but she can't be found. And the man in black
has lost his face in his hands.
Their nursery rhyme
their folk tale
is everywhere. But what is it?
What can I do
but touch your hand and hope
my hands aren't cold.

Houdini (the river, his chains)
knew how to live. And Santa Teresa lived
her visions, her love of plainness.
It is somewhere within the voice
and if the voice is mute
that also is a cry. The deep silence before
the birth of language, after the death of sounds
is what makes the harp sing
and the wind rise.

Home Improvement

Dogs and cats, he said, they ain't that different.
Both front loaders and both dump from the rear.
Good machines you ask me, cats and dogs.
Course you can train a dog but no damn cat.

As to trainin I got to France with the boys on D-Day.
Survived on Omaha because I knew
just when to cut and run and head for cover.
How deep you want me to cut this driveway now.

Had a dog once could eat cats. Nothin left
of the cat but an old helmet with a hole in it.
That was some cat too. Cats never give up.
Not like some boys you got to train to fight.

I'll get my nephew to saw down them cedar trees.
The worst fightin we did was in the Ardennes
couldn't see nothin. Went at it cats and dogs
and Lord knows what other crap thrown in besides.

Still I'm alive ain't I. Should take about a week
to get that drive graded proper. That old dozer there
ain't exactly a Sherman. That your dog I see
staring out at me from that jasmine bush

or is it a big old cat? I reckon it could take
another week before we get to Berlin.
That is if it don't rain and the ground ain't hard.
We'll talk about the cost when we get there, friend.

Le Sacre

A bird's flight like a sudden catch of breath
is how spring begins. In the warm south
it comes loudly and suddenly. The light
was always there, the soft white eye
lay open just under the grass watching us.

I am my body and blood take eat and
remember me. We share our old house
as the birds own the air, precariously.
No wind today. The lake is very still.
I climb the lake with tentative hands and feel

the cold of new air, the chill
just under spring. I remember being young in the north
and have always somehow feared the worst
the long wait above the slow life of water
released at last like grief.

In the south as Lorca said
it is so often in spring that the coffins appear
the dead borne into sunlight after winter
and planted as new seeds.
The old ones I remember went like that

the long processions wound uphill and
down again as we watched, or walked with them
quickly, not slowly, as the custom was
never to linger. In the south
the sun and wind and light are decorous

and there is no long brooding except
shadows sometimes watch you. I open my hand
and find them now. They have names
or they had names. Some were too close
like you, and some too distant to be remembered

though they are all here
the light a soft gray, the smell like rain.
What can I give of myself I sometimes
wonder to forgive myself these lives.
Too much and too small a rite of sacrifice.

A bird's flight like a sudden catch of
breath in the throat is how spring ends.
The south wind blows now. A blue metallic wasp
with amber wings is hunting the screen for spiders
above my desk.
The heat we share, hers fierce.

Abstract

A piece of cloth, a quality of shadow.
The Aryan clause that meant
no Jew could find work, or a baby
curled at the she-wolf's feet
whining for milk, milk, time to think.

The scream where silence lingered
a moment too long
as paper thins with reading, thins
and what is left is air, a pressure on the eye
or behind the eye, a memory of old song

the future has no sound for.
She wears your clothes, she moves from room to room
in a gallery of white-filled squares.
Unlettered whiteness, like a sacred book
no one has opened for centuries.

When I look into your future eyes
I see this shadow, waiting like snow in the wind.
White noise … White silence … perhaps a reason to live.
If it matters the poetry will come.
If it matters, I say, the poem will be there.

Old Age

I found some chewing gum.
Gum, I said, what *are you* chewing?
Nothing but air, said gum.
The teeth are gone.

Night Bus South

I might have imagined the voices singing.
To our left, a pressure of hillside
lights of Monterrey and the higher stars
paler, just as close. So when the song
came to me, riffling through your hair
like a vision of night insects without wings
I thought the voices were only part of your dream
a bend in the road south, day waiting for us
ahead, in a new country. Then I wondered
if the night wind – or was it just one
of many possible sounds – had let me remember
a younger journey, alone, away from one
whose hands are now cold: a blood song of dead stars
I touch in your wrist, its pulse alive, still warm.

Altiplano

The tragic absence of rivers

what is it so moves me in the wind

the long wailing chord of noonday light

The Mystery

They said of my father: George was a good man.
They said of my mother: Sylvia was a saint.
But the people who said that sort of thing
are now almost gone. I recall
the bread they baked, the white aprons
the pipesmoke caught in wool, and those
long winters the bones never forget
that turn to names and dates engraved in stone.
Sometimes I thank God I never
knew my parents, yet loved them, and was loved.
Among the normal torments of being a child
I didn't need the griefs they hid from me.
What I am now lies in shadow. Could I, should I
speak of two dead lovers as my wound?

Daylight Saving

Who can get it up
on a cold morning
afraid of the day facing him
in the windowlessness before dawn.
What are the cats doing
out there in the grass
or the old dog pretending to sleep
on her bed of dry leaves
under the dead oak tree
as the last train clears the station
dragging itself away
from the furious white inferno
that had been our beloved city
children without families now
crying to me to be their father
so many hands gripping mine
I must lose count. Why
regret these lives that seek you
who seek themselves
and are only shadows.
What you have never known
will haunt you forever.
What you are
are hands reaching for yours
in the namelessness
of something's desperate need.
And these pathetic games
go down with the rising sun
your inscrutable permission to live.

On a Monday in April

Sometimes the passageways, lined with doors
reveal younger faces. I saw you as a child
watching from the shadow of her mother
while the dapple fingerlings of April leaves
played, like naked swimmers' bodies
warm, cold, alive in my hand. In
San Miguel the streets knelt uphill
gazing up at the blue dusty sky
where bells were waiting to roll downhill
on heavy broken wheels. Face by face
the hours of birth of spring in these passageways
cry for time, more time. They have cold hands.
I read in their eyes the wildness
of what will never happen, the secret names.

April, a Memo

The east wind off center
tracking, my eyeglasses
lost, while April bees
licking at high-rise windows
make it rain so suddenly
the turtle that lay in me
all winter is out
its sharp beak mowing
the sea that touches my feet
so lightly it's air
crying *murder* in Serbo-Croat
testing the sunlight, wind
one finger raised
and the memory of you
your blue skirt spread on grass
orphaned at last
by the lives you gave birth to
who then went on
or stopped like yours.

Chelmno, Poland, Winter 1941

What can we save from the forest?
Eyes, maybe. Shoes with watchful eyes
that froze when the gas trucks came for us
the first day, tracing the snow
like a task in geometry. Suddenly
the air sickened. I thought of spring flowers
my mother had gathered. They also
she said had eyes. But it was December
a time to praise God and whatever
spirits the trees kept secret from our prayers.
Half a century gone, I keep their names
none of the faces. Can the forest save
us? We the dead
and we the living have stiffened
folded our arms, settled our limbs
curled up, gone thin and silent.
Though some of us rise up off the snow
in triumph crying *Honor us, honor the shoes that*
walked us here, the caps, the kerchiefs, coats
or in the white dusk *Come back, don't abandon us*
nephew as his thin-boned ghost
drifted off through the quiet trees. And
always, suddenly, wasn't there anymore.

Beyond

Night of south winds! night of the large few stars!
Walt Whitman's voice crying out
to Pablo Neruda in Isla Negra, Chile
a hundred years beyond. But tonight

I press my ear against the soft bark
of a dying live-oak tree. Its roots are remote,
silent: they confess no pain, they
have no voices. What to save

what to let go. White, edgy leaves
scattered like manna across the grass.
I put on the tree's age, I wait for sunrise

about which it knew so much and so little.
I gaze beyond at the far, light-flecked hills.
The homes there are worth millions.

New Year's Day Wedding
For Shan and Germán

Who's gone away
taking something with her
we do not miss yet
though there is this preparation
to receive her absence like
a guest, a new daughter
in an old familiar house
none of us can picture
prepare a manger, a room
a language she must learn
to be free of us
starting then, beginning
now with this wedding
the red, the white, off-white
on this deck among winter flowers
her words, his words
and all our watching hearts
and the thought continues
the endless thought goes on.

Yellow Flowers out in January

The weak sun struggles through cloud
but these whims are never wrong
however fatal. You
are what keep us alive
when the quiet voice warns us.

Tortoise Shell

All the old roofs of the world
brushed by wind the dull hollow harp
and taste of bitter thick coffee
the heat of summer days a lost
Panzer half buried in North African sand
this house that still attaches us
by sinews and blood long after
the years of invasion and defeat
the years spent hiding in cellars
for friendlier helmets to summon us out
into a blue air filled with smoke
of cigarettes not cannon fire
and this one made it through motherhood
possibly   laid her young in the sand
by this dirt road used by few cars
for my fingers to walk her rooms
and guess the tenant's history from these scars.

Old Families

They are the ones the future will think of
as intimate friends; the enemies we hate
came later and were anonymous. Meanwhile
we try hard to improve our lives
to raise our sons and daughters as we would
raise corn if the land was ours. The birds
bring us news. It is comforting to know
that church spire on the horizon still stands
as our storm compass, our dry lightning rod.
In city centers we touch our mouths softly
and feel the old wind singing, an old song
whose syllables are the empty shells of snails
whose sentences are miles and miles of fenceline
which are the names we keep and keep forgetting.

Ethnic Poem III

As the sun begins to bend over the hill
around the trees and the early summer heat
pushes the dry cloud-killing wind
ahead of it, the shadowy migrations
of a people. They do not want to leave
my sight. For days they have wandered south
and south and west ahead of the bitter men
with knives and rifles. The tall ones lean
heavily then lightly on one another and then
fall down and lie there, and the eye has no time
to harm or help them. I will live as before
without accomplishment. I will begin to praise
the compassion of witnesses, go as the river flows
with lives borne downstream always vanishing.

Old Teacher

There are too many unknowns in the equations
and white chalk on black can slip into negative
at any moment. Truly it is the reverse
of a line one might write to a lover or friend
and so little is new. It is these faces
that slowly turn back into names, that learn
or fail to learn his voice, so when his day ends
nothing stirs in the room but a neutral dust
waiting for moonlight when chalk comes alive
as a white dry thin song. It is then
after the erasure of all the numbers and signs
that the beauty of the whole becomes transparent
and too clear to describe. As in a rare dream
the perfect poem or that faint lost chord
comes suddenly to mind, and he must tell everyone
that he was their generation's promised saviour
wandering in no Holy Land but time
in exile from the eyes that cannot hear him
the mouths that spit on him that scream that scream.

A Window in London

Who was that you saw walk past
turn and stare at you and go on walking
up the street to the left of your eye
then returns and stares right up at you
while you hide behind the curtain edge
not afraid but unwilling to be found
your eye gone inward now, the square
of autumn leaves the beginning of cold winds
imagining a figure seen through glass
looking not for you but for her now
and how do you say she is gone
before the horns of winter and the cold
catch her, the flick of a lighter at a
cigarette the room gone much too quiet
and the stranger prowling across your eye
how will you get rid of him
what will you do do with yourself.

Bad Ghosts

I say the words lightly
as one might say
the milk's off, or the day
gone dark too early. Do not
look at them. They have your eyes
mother, they have your mouth.
They hear you coming and wait
where the four winds cross
where the light cancels itself.
I say this lightly, as one
who has had to learn a new speech
(the old had too many echoes)
and to care for something, some one
is to risk keeping them alive
is to feed their hunger with mine.
I can never be sure
which one of them you were.
I risk not knowing my shame.

Saeta

If you asked me where the village was
I would have to say, I remember it
but it has changed, the sun has aged
infinitesimally these twenty years
and so have the shadows. The young have grown
new young, and who are left of the old ones
I remember as younger. They fought
and lost in Franco's war, in Lorca's war.
Their bodies bend and twist and cling
to hillsides, and in the end
they enter a wall set with flowers and candles.
The shadow and body are never separate.
Like an old man and woman they bend
and shuffle and sweep the leaves from their feet.

Night Clouds

If in my life there were two people
I wish I had never met, that
was a tragedy. What happened then
had mapped itself out in the stars
which are character, it appears
and no one could change or undo
what hopelessly was done. I have rested
my head too long and often on this rock
which has taken the shape of my skull
and no journey, *grass for a pillow*
of adventure or escape felt quite right.
Griefs held too long go to bone, or stone.
Only one day the light may seem different
and a new star shine with the morning sun.

Elzbieta

My dog shapes her mouth into an anus
and howls. If I put my finger in there
the howling stops, the dog looks desperate.
Why take from her the one song she sings
perfectly, the long note of the wolf
softened to a contralto, but her voice
her response to the metallic false cry
of fire or police in our rural neighbourhood
I ask myself. At night it is like
a brown wind passing through summer fur
or on the coldest nights like a lost star
crying to be named. Where did she come from
five Novembers ago, no longer young
so overweight and with that foolish grin.

Three Daughters

It is hard not to repeat myself
each of you being the one you are
the one she is, as clear and different
as any three mirrors. You move
under all my words, you have moved
what I have become. If this is less
than eloquence forgive me. There are
days left there is paper left to try again.
So much has happened to you so much can
happen still. A finger at a time
an eye a nose a lip you entered your names
and make them dance. It is like
the circling of music around one note
that repeats itself and is never thrice the same.

Vigil

I was walking alone uphill
with my car on my back
when the car became a backpack
and somewhere I lost it. Child
I had warned her long ago
the minute you spread your wings you risk
disturbing some god. Look here
at this refuse of old books
the kind no one would read
the kind you find in old hotels
in colonial towns, shelved behind glass
while waiting for someone to come
who said she'd meet you here
but is late. And the light grows old.

Above the Mediterranean

Along those aqueducts in the hills
the cold melted mountain snows
and blood of Moor and Roman ground
to infinitesimally fine
scratchings of soil. But we
keep house with breadcrumbs and spiders.
The stone jug mouth bends
curls toward the fountain to drink
the dry earth whose cold mouth quenches us.
In the shadow of that hill at night they pass us
the seed-bearers of time, two anonymous runners.

Montserrat

Closed in your hand a child
we talk about sometimes
her name already chosen. Now
in July, the shadow of the human tree
in the heat her seed still sleeps.

At her temple in the cold a star shines.
Shines against the fierce mask of the sun
though her house is still dark

dark as you imagine her
eyes watchful, from the dark watching like
a water star, like a dream's faint chance to live.

La Vida

When Loli trimmed her cat's whiskers
we told her, Loli, cats need those
to finger their way through life.

But Loli was young and hadn't thought
why cats are cats and how
some day her own whiskers would grow

and keep her from bumping into things
with names like Juan Antonio
and Paco and José and Manolito.

Citlanicue (Star Mother)

Mother wash your hands in the sun
the sun will burn them, burn them clean
you leave us these few bones
your calcium is good for us
your ash would be no use to us.

This bright morning I have been
sleepless since early dark
the sun not yet up over the
right-hand mountain, one day left in June
fires on the dry ground
and in all the windows a
blank look

expectant, like a woman about to give
voice to a thought no man has ever dreamed.

Tlalteuctli (Earth Lady)

Out of your hair the trees the tall grasses
out of your skin the flowers the little grass
out of your eyes the springs
from your mouth the rivers and caves
from your wide nose the valleys
from your round shoulders the mountains

great toad with open mouths where your limbs are joined
each mouth dribbling blood
the coiled snakes crushed and cut you in two pieces
your upper body the sky
your lower body the earth
O we pitied you and watered you

we cried for water from your breasts
you gave us your milk we took it all wrong.

An Event About to Happen

It was taken in the late afternoon
by a steadier hand than mine.
There is a smell of late snow
and cold patches of thawed grass
her shoes are wet with it.
The tree she leans against is an oak.
Distance is caught behind her
like a long rope thrown over a wooden post
the afternoon still against the blue sea waves
some marlin fishermen running for open water.
My hand brushes this mirror, touches
a blue dress hung out to dry
at the season's cold edge
waiting for someone to claim it
or disown it. I imagine wind
riffling the branches of her hair
as the oak tree waits for its leaves.
Her name leaves no shadow. The sea
the fishermen are far away now.
There is no cry. There is no negative.

Bettelheim

I had finished washing up
wiped my hands and turned the light down low
when the trees west of the house appeared to move
slowly as if following the sun down
the farthest woods that let them filter through
trailing their hands to be touched
one by one, and I heard
human names. And a phrase *the terrible silence
of children* came to me from a book
the work of an old man who died
touched white with grace and suffering
if that is ever a grace. And I wondered
how many of those silent survivors ever found
themselves. For the dead they couldn't mourn
there can only be remembrance and yet
the children of those who disappeared
their eyes like empty spaces the trees left
in the cold abstraction of grief why can't we
speak to them? I mistook
the ghosts of children for the shapes of trees
trees for the shadows of children
tree-ghost, child-ghost, selves lost in selves.
And I am haunted by a need to forgive
and be forgiven that cries beyond my voice
to the silence of children whose lost names
are the dead who hide beneath these words.

Soltera

In my house there is always a child crying
she said, as if the poetry
weren't good enough. At night
what I take to be rain is only the wind.
What is it that is not there
and is there and lives between the doors
and windows of things between
the mountains and the sea
like a white cross on the top of a hill
something to focus the heart
when all else drifts off towards a silence.

Spirit

Homer my black and white
female cat lies in the grass
just off the edge of the sun
in the shade of a hackberry.
The breeze that flickers in the grass
unsettles her summer-thin fur
above her the cries of cardinals
one to the other. The day is not yet hot
but this is Texas. Her cat mind
entertains a silence of its own.
It includes the nibbling of squirrels
it watches with pale eyes
the yellow tom approach across the grass
who is a stranger and who shares her food.
What follows resembles sleep
except for a feathering of her ears
slight as an impatience in the wind.

Ethnic Poem IV

When she spread out her arms she touched
the air of a wall. It had been there
forever she thought as a knife edge of shadow
cut between her fingers and her mind.
There were friendly eyes behind the windows.
They spoke like her and thought like her
and had her children's names. The hills
that always told her the time of day
were angry with her now. There were
no clocks or calendars left, but
shell-bursts in the wind cut slices of time
into keener fractions than the winter ice.
Nothing would hurt her. Who could desire
a woman so bruised, so old, so bitter to taste.

Summer Storms

The last few winter fire logs
stacked by the overgrown path up to the house
sun and shadow dapple, spider webs.
Hard to know the mood of summer days.
She listens and nothing answers. She
shouts angrily for help at the stuck screen door
to the kitchen. She kicks and screams
that life is terrible for her and then
calms down having gotten all that done.
He retreats into the way it has always felt
to be too quiet, neither dark nor fair
in the light of the witness's camera
that stares at them from the sun. Somewhere
an eye widens in pain, a poem gathers.

Trespassers

Are you what the tide gathered.
This far inland it is common
to imagine the sea where somehow
you drifted up and I gathered you
we gathered each other and kept ourselves.
The river that is our neighbour flows
south through slums and rice fields to where
the land brightens and darkens
at the edge of the Rio Grande
that separates our lives. I would
come there to hear your voice
play across your past like a thin hand
like a seashell keeping a song. Why is it
so hard for me to know why this is hard for you.

Those Childish Sundays

I used to think the Lamb of God
meant Jesus had a stuffed toy
he could play with and talk to
while Mary was otherwise occupied
and Joseph busy making shelves. That
I thought was the ideal family
everyone about his own business and no one
lonely or left out. Then to learn
that the lamb was an abstraction was terrible.
The whole picture fell apart
like a bad marriage with a custody battle
over the child. The last I heard
they were living out near Nazareth
in separate flats, and the boy was into God.

In Late June

But for the tapping of a hammer on wood
the light is going nowhere, the green
of the early sun fired to near white
in the elm leaves. A few old
dry ones flitter down into the too-long grass.
Birds waiting before the heat to come
talk quietly about personal matters
secrets I try to distill from words
that have no song or color and can't fly.
It is sometime late in life. I am here
at this moment. I am here and every place
and moment I have ever been is here.
The wind rises, the disorder of quiet air
reaches for me, and I breathe again.

Primo Levi

The answer one was always looking for
was one's life. And if the lives of others
became your life, so they were no longer
themselves but were also your shadows who
you were desperate to feed but couldn't save
until it was too late for you, then
that promise you kept. *It is easier*
you said *to deny entry to*
a memory than to free oneself from it
after it has been recorded. Your courage then
was to redeem your many deaths for the sake of us
who'd lived and not lived where their cry took root.
Was it your record of those lives and deaths
that freed you at last. Or was it the memory.

Chihuahua

Sunlight litters the hills. Across all
walkways of the desert something has moved
and is now motionless. It is still
too early to feel the pain of heat.
Creatures who live with the sun, that is
who live in shadow, the small loose stones
tell them we are coming. Some of us
can live without sex and some without water
and they are the ones who travel light
who live in the vivid margins of old scrolls
or dry up like parchment. The lizard child
has no time for his shadow, his old self.
Grace here flickers from one stone to the next
and emerges at the end with a huge cold thirst.

Conversation

I have this habit of talking to you
when you're not there. Your absence gives me time
to explain why it is I love silence
as much as you need voices. When
we are together the silence tilts towards you
and takes your name and eyes. It
leaves me and becomes your need to remember
something important, something perhaps very small
that being forgotten has the power to kill
us both. I knock three times on wood
for the shadow who lives in our bones
grants three wishes. The first is memory.
The second is that the secret you remember
is worth your life. The third one has no face.

Fragment

When the wind blows from the south
it bears the south's light with it
and the trees begin their long walk in the sky
north to this window. I am the book
whose pages the wind flickers through
too quickly to read. I am the knowledge
of myself lost in the quickness of its hands.

Possession

The antique Mexican straw hat
has a dried *serrano* pepper tied to its brim
with a knot of fishing line. The hat
is heavy. When I put it on I feel
the whole weight of the sun on the earth
pressing me down. I bend
and kneel in the dirt and begin to dig
with my hands. With all four hands
I dig a shallow hole, smelling for water.
The sun on my back is like the lash
of a master. The hat begins to spread
like a great carob tree, its heavy shade
surrounds me like the circle of an eye.
I have found the center of the earth.

Energy

The effort, the always struggle with the dark
that begins at your eyes. The fear
that gives you heart. So restless that
nothing can ever be this thing you wanted
no place the hoped for paradise
and you keep trying. I am moved
by this one close to me so driven
like a thousand pages scattered in the wind
each with your name, your inaudible signature
crying to be heard yet so afraid of that.

Heatwave

It is these nights when
the work of being alive goes on
long after the sun has gone
and you yourself are the shriek of the cicada
when after the light has gone
the heat of the solid dark
cries within your cells and will not
scratch or wash off. It is
waiting for the hours of the pale clock
to fall exhausted into another dream
like the one of lying awake
imagining Paris and Helen hot
in the archaic night of far clearer stars
that lit their way from breath
to breath at the cold end of desire.
It is the way you lie there
waiting to be picked and eaten whole.

Ethnic Poem V

There are so few of us who ever learn
how few we are. *Mother* the child said
it's so dark, it's so dark
and I was being so good. The voice
can only be remembered in the words
as if you heard them, but you never heard them.
The door did not close on your eyes
that closed upon the voice. You read the words
now and imagine the voice of a child you heard
in a bus queue or at the dentist's office
complaining. It is the same kind of voice
but not that door. To pass through the door
that shut forever you must imagine a child
just like that but with its father's eyes.

Ottawa, April 1964

They bring her water at night
but she can't help asking what the wind is like
and if the world is still everywhere
she thought it was. The days
beginning now are white and thin as paper.
On each one is written her name
over and over again in ink that fades
as the light catches it. Her children
do not own her now, nor does her man.
It is like the slow dream of a violin
lying in its case, the music is
all hers now, no one else can hear her.
Bless this one who others call a saint
that she remain a woman, and die as one.

Poet's Poet

Having drunk so much beer
he could hardly feel his legs
he opened his fly and released
his stream of consciousness into the wind
and it blew back at them
and the critics loved it.

South Wind

When the south rises it is rebellious
and the north must restore order
or our lives are in danger. The photo
is old but clear. Villa and Zapata
relax on upholstered chairs, they
have just taken the Capital. Their
deep straw hats are like dry wells, what
can they talk about that does not anger them
the hard days the long waiting in line
for a warm *peso* from the foreman's pocket
that brittles and turns thin
when the air touches it. Now
the slow eye of the camera lends them time.
Memory is a long wind. Behind
their eyes another wind is rising.
The bullets turn to feathers in the air.

Genesis

I hold the ant between my thumb and finger
and feel it struggle. It is
a giant of its kind. Nothing I do
can do more than crush out its life.
Behind it are all the demons of the sun
milling in their hidden nests. My time
is precious. I am the life I hold.

Wait

The camera had missed your face.
We watched you as you closed your eyes
as if the light were tired. You smiled
and turned your better profile to the sun.

A man behind me kept trying to
say something. Don't fall asleep on us, he joked.
Your profile and the sun's face blent in a kiss.
There were no features left. Just fire, and time.

Now the man behind me had gone.
A girl-child started crying in someone's arms.
A shutter clicked. The child stopped.
The tree where you'd been standing turned to wind.

Then winter, now fall. It seems
there is still a lot of explaining to be done.
The wind hangs in the tree. And I am gone.
The child is gone. And you were late, but perfect.

The Cemetery of the Nameless

A pure wind blows across
the cemetery of the nameless.
It is not words, or voices.
The hands of the trees here call for silence
and in the little pauses between winds
the rain gathers. The rain
is ourselves gathering. And soon a car
starts up and we all follow it home.
Afterward is when night becomes hard.

In the line between your eyes
there burned a filament of anger.
The afternoon grows colder now. The cemetery
lies west of the city, is hard to reach
by bicycle or on foot, flowers to bear
in summer even, when the fanatical light
whitened our green world. Now
in the cool incandescence of this fall
we hold ourselves upright, hands in pockets

and leap across tiny streams
with the stiff agility of children grown old.
Family after family the dry names
cry and fall. Red, yellow, brown names
gone in the darkening of a single hour.
We were lovers once, remember? sings
the last voice in the air beyond the rain.
Aloft like a Habsburg coachman
in nothing but a tall black hat

filtered through sunlit yellow hackberry leaves
the wind blows, shapely and dark.

Mournfully and in haste
your voice comes mocking: *You never tried*
to find me. You never asked anyone
where I went and hid myself, against the rain.
But now we are all the same crowd.
We walk in this anonymity
of gray wind, the sudden lack of voices

crying behind us the names of all their lives.
My words are infected because I was there.
I knew her says the tall man in a
black coat, cheating again. Among
the stones lie the ones who survive us
and though we would weep for them
we cannot. For they are ourselves
and we never knew them while the broken mirror
kept their breath. Tomorrow they say

there will be rain and more rain.
There will be leaf and leaf and leaves falling.
Leaves and lovers and all the old designs
to enthrall and kill them. Throughout
the grand empire where your people once lived
there are signs of mourning in all the villages.
And some of us will cry out

and some of us say nothing
because the words will seem cheap
and the words will not rise to a voice
to sing or tell a story you can trust.
There is no use lamenting
for what is lamentable is anonymous
and always personal. Acts, names left out
or censored from the memoir, from the poem
so memory is forever its own ghost

and falls as rain, and dries as rain.
Listen again. Tell me where you are.

In the room next door
a man is reading, alone.
He is mourning the life of someone
he hardly knew, a woman
and the afternoon is darkening outside
leaving his hands in shadow on the table.
The crowds in the streets are going home.
Among the feathers, hats, umbrellas, coats
two naked children are running and kissing the wind.

Pied Piper

Waking up cold in a strange room
where the bed is hard and the light
comes from an unfamiliar window, this
is some place on the way to where
I set out years ago though I
have forgotten the name and have only
my own name for every city and town
that talks my language. The rats
are no bigger, the children no different
and I never vary my tune, though the cry
gets wilder, the pipe a pitch more shrill
as my temper thins. In these times
I always say, in these times
one must take no chances.

My Father's Hand

His long fingers touch my head
tentatively, rest there a moment
then return to him. He wanted
to look at me but was it his heart
that did that. It was a voice
a gesture he felt in my name
his son, his name, that his eye
could not look at directly or mouth
say easily. That touch
I have with me as the sun wind or rain
on my head whenever I walk
in an unfamiliar place where the long street
seems to want to lead me to its end
not visible through the fierce light and dust.

Summer Morning for Felicity

You must get up as early as the light
a fine tremor that is more like water
a tolerance of the air, early morning.
Your eyes have waited all night
to open. Your eyes have waited all night
to come to life. You see the world
you saw fifty years ago but had
no words for. Having the words
now makes the light hold still a moment
and the moment resembles your life
as a dry leaf hangs and spins on a thread
of web off an elm twig. A mile away
the sound of a truck engine revving
burls through the river valley
like the sudden memory of forgetting
a name whose life depended on your own.
And memory and light seem identical
the calm witness come to detect again
a look in your eyes, a child's question
asking what day it is, an aging man
or a woman afraid of growing old
while the light speaks to her. You see
what the trees could always have told you
if the wind had left them the words
if the light had given them mouths.

SOLO WITH GRAZING DEER

2001

*Presence is just a special case
in the category of absence.*
        —Roberto Calasso, KA

*Deer graze here each morning
for you harm nothing.*
        —Du Fu

The River That Drowned

Years ago when I was a child in Japan
there were no seasons I can remember.
There were always soldiers in the streets
and children wore black uniforms to school.

In our high garden above the valley
of small houses, I was at home. There
were Christmases, the birth of a sister
parties with paper hats, lawn tennis, skiing

in the winter mountains. By then
the armies were deep in China, towns were burning.
I remember helping the gardener, my friend
wind the khaki cloth puttees around his shins

before he went off to drill in a dusty field
below the house. I was at war
with no one, only the English neighbour boy
who'd come to play and hogged my favourite toys.

There are films my father made recording
some of this. I rescued what I could
of the old 16mm reels, cracked, spliced
and faded, and had them compressed to a brief

video memento. The wide-eyed child my self
survives there in a world his parents remembered
too fondly to ever feel quite whole again
in the deeper snows of Canada we came to

before the armies moved south out of China
before the murders in Asia, the bombs on
Hawaii, the killings back westward across
the islands, the last incredible fires.

Lamp

While I was dreaming inside my flame
the wind bit at the edges of my teeth
and I thought I could see in the dark –
it was your word against mine.

Though they had broken shattered pieced together
Dresden and Hiroshima
Coventry London Guernica
the shadows you left wouldn't move.

So in Robert Capa's photograph
of a street in Bilbao in 1936
eight women and men and a young girl
look up at the sky at where German bombers

are coming. So it might have been
a little before dawn when a boy not quite one
woke up in a white crib in Yokohama
and saw shadows cross the ceiling of his room

– the world had soft bones
and old and brittle bones
and from time to time the light falls
exactly where the body runs to hide.

Sabi

I feel my rust beginning.
It is inside me and between my fingers
a slow cold itching, like distant rain.
Or brown eating at the edge of a leaf
which is the light withdrawing
the mirror withheld
the air's child that hides.

The sun tests the future with a tentative hand.
I know the gender of water, the cold
beginning of memory under the long evening light
that comes to no fulfilment but itself.
The light that keeps returning has no language.
I am content to remember how you breathed.

Memory and Season

Somewhere between here and Japan, the summer wind rises
as delicate as a salad made by her hands.
It was a loss of heart we were thinking about
when pain killed the child too far away.
How often, brother, lying under the stars
you have returned to now, how often and
in all fairness did her soft cry warn us
too soon or too late?

Rune

Under the wind there is a place where you can hide.
Think of it as a silent event. An evening comes,
and you are ready to tell a story you have never
heard, tell it in such a way that whatever secrets
you had gather around you now to listen. They have
no name but yours, and they are still listening.

The High Cold Air

My brother, there are just
bones under the skin, as if
air had entered and dried up
the rest of him. As if
the driest of winds had cracked through
and stolen the water
so he died of thirst
not cancer, but thirst

So what of this skeleton leaf
gone but for the thin pattern of veins

And the girl they call Juanita
under that high mountain ice
kept preserved, knees
to chin, neck bent, eyes gone
what name can bring her to life
can comb her long hair with its hand
whisper that life is good
so good?

Landscape

In autumn the silences grow loud.
The sounds become echoes.
I have been gone a long time, they
changed my number, the branch
I hung from has been cut.
In the room the shadow dolls
play across bare walls, there are
fresh spiders. The music I heard came
from outdoors, celebrations of air, wind
rain, at the ear's edges, listening.
Why won't you come in? A traffic
of handcars running along rails over
loose coals. An engine starting stops
abruptly. The silence is like a brush across
dry canvas, like slow fingers playing
through pubic hair. A white cat sits
like a harp on the window sill. It is
cold in the mountains, after a summer
training my eyes to see
what they once remembered. I note
the place where my chair stood
a square of pale light on the grey
carpet. What would you like to do?
The soup kitchen, the popular *sushi* bar
usually fill by noon. The river
below is the colour and chill
of fish, my fingers go numb
winding and unwinding this wet string.
You used to play an elegant piano.
Now in the place where the piano was
a crowd of echoes cries circling
desperately to find your hands. We are

out of touch. A sudden dash of rain
wets the glass and moves on. Tires
in the street exhale through wet teeth.
You were impatient with me. Three
seasons out of four the room chose colours
we both liked, heights of canyons brushed
with a first snow, brown shadowed by deep
green in the conifers just before dawn.
The patch of shadow where night
lay still in your armpit, a smell
like riverweed a moment out of water.
The almost white room is
emptying now. It is a book with blank pages
or a book whose familiar pages have faded
to this. There is no eloquence like
whiteness and silence. There are no
words where words end. The
room is empty now and white with shadows.
Black forest against white mountains
far away. A lone crow flying.

Revenant

Too far within the eye
the smell of conifer wind, hot summer wood.

To outlive your childhood
the needy flies, the knee-deep water
rivering over the heads of soft stones.

Give a thought to the age
of things I've touched, always
the blessing of forgetfulness

in the heat of the city
the captive memory wind killing time.

Or there is what doesn't use its hands
to lift itself. Out of the chilled stream
into her young rose mouth
opening like numbers. Lost

moments, opportunities. The
names of some gone to seed in their lives
as I have (you have) mine.

What I see can only stretch beyond itself
into the shadows of futures
as things were then. The
sunlight feels closer now

because the only shadow is mine.
It took all those years to get here.

May Month
For Isabela

Why do I feel suddenly happy?
I must have been happy all along, and didn't know it.
Is this possible?

Of the homes I have abandoned.
There are trees that never see the sun
but they carry the memory of suns.

Out of the grass steps a bird with no wings.

The youngest one here
blows out two candles.

Her voice is only a breath. Between
two wishes a scar grows over an old wound
as gentle as an eye approaching evening.

Whish! the bird has flown.

Blue Roofs

Antlers of white cloud
high to the north.
Bands of winter.

I remember one thing I should not
have forgotten. White times two,
an absence of mind.

Thinking to understand what cost her
her life, abstractions
of distance now, haiku

spelling their way from the sun
into my open hand,
rain snow snow

beginnings of blue.
Somewhere, how,
the bones gather to sing

in an empty ashtray, a deep well,
this lessening of hunger
as the years become sufficient

to themselves. Or am I saying
that white must be perfection,
a clean plate, a light without a source

the failure to remember your smell
a hiding of every colour
memory crying for water.

Caravans

The weather is old.
Feathers of words drift
between rains, time
of Ovid watching the Black Sea

wanting home. But that
was his story. The rain
lifts, and someone's face
is watching you, still

for just this moment
without expression, like the sea's edge
where children were playing
only yesterday. Ships

came and went
carrying messages the rain
dissolved. Forgive me, they read.
I am penitent, let me return.

Years pass, but never completely
lose us. Pass like ancient skirts
of dancing bears and caravans
in the mud between rains. Death

was fire and the rains
extinguished it. Never
exile when your own shadow falls
foot by mile by plot along

the weather's old roads.
The words were harsh feathers
that scratched at your throat
in the dust between rains. Dry

not tears. No grief
like old grief settled deep
under the stony earth, deeper than
where rains can loosen it. Bodies

not names. Not histories where
the letters get lost or misread
in lives which were fires until
the rains extinguished them. The

bright skirts and the caravans
passing. The poet crying for his mother
tongue at the sea's edge, not
lost, but found. Between

rains a face you never saw before
watching you try to recognize
yourself. The mirror at the sea's edge
between rains lifts its eyes.

贝

I am drawn to *bèi,* the Chinese cowrie radical
in its simplified form, how it resembles
a hidden man stepping out cautiously
in the shadow of his hood, off to the right
as all characters move to the right
if they move at all. Cowrie shells
were money in ancient China. The figure occurs
in keeping with things of value, commerce, trade.
But I think of him walking the streets alone
night and day, with no thought but to hide himself
like Camus' stranger or Eliot's compound ghost
the masked spirit of some truth whose voice
and silence keep the broken sun from rising
too soon for us, who choose his company.

Piscean Song

I have run away so often
turned my back
I am like the road

I have abandoned so many
places and been left for dead
in houses that went dark

and there are some half-dozen
faces I regret whose names
are holes left in my mind

holes that begin to fill
slowly with dark water
reflecting nothing

though occasionally on clear nights
the stars lean down
they say that memory is time

time now and little else
gone farther and farther away
my mirror that lies to me
my soft voice no one answers

The sea curls and curls
and I am taken away
always from where I have been.

Stump

The burnt-out house we are always
afraid of. One open
upstairs room made over to the
voices of stars, a song
beyond itself returning to our ears.

In the beginning the shadows of our hands
played with us, the shapes
of light before our bodies could crawl.
I remember the old stump
where the tree was. Darker clothes
that hid my mother's face. The
soft laundry folded by the years.

When we were young
the answers were what we touched.
The grain of words was something less than paper
more than the wind. The rain
brings me to you. The rain that
precedes fire, that soaks the hard dirt road.

We all rise too early
or we sleep too late. The
golden grain we ran through down to the valley
is the texture of a painting. Where the
roof was, where the stars
kill time. I have

trouble now imagining where I belonged
and in what season, whose house this is.
My grandchild's eyes are bright water drops
in the night sky. She is new to us.
We hold to what we have. We hold hold.

Railroad Tracks, House for Sale and Clouds

She left us while the light was bad.
A sudden movement on the hill, pepper
shaken from heavy clouds.

Someone kept asking, who?
But in a voice I didn't understand
like rain in a dry field, remotest echo.

The sweep of the long field slightly uphill
framed by two eucalyptus in the midground.
SE VENDE ESTA CASA. Silence of afternoon.

And the tracks long long ago abandoned.
Grey deliberate rails from left to right
and back again, the eye the only pilgrim.

From left to right and back again
across the high, brown, dry sun-tipped grass.
Like her mind, like that dead tree.

Or the other one fallen on the roof
too frail to break the tiles, or the hill line
beyond, where we saw her move.

And the clouds darkening now,
the fire at their edges softer, gone.
Snow in the Andes. Hail on the lower fields.

How memory brings us to a place
then hides like that, leaving not even a name.
I call and hear nothing but holes.

Happiness

No one goes to the park in winter.
Quiet hands, eyes, there is little to speak of.
Absence is a colour not a sound.

Unless when the sound dies it becomes
the colour white, as in a Chinese story
by Lu Hsun from which the opening line

of this poem comes. There a thin man
a good teacher who lost his job, a misanthrope
who loved only children, died

spitting blood, like a red sound on the snow
white of Chinese death. So this park
where I think the two of us walked once

I've forgotten if we ever came here but
we lived close by, whatever the season was
it returns to me now as a place filled with voices

I thought were ours. I open this book
and the pages turn to leaf and winterbrown grass.
Over it all broods the distant waking sun.

February

I stood on the back deck and then
a jewel of a moon came up and hung
among the branches. They seemed closer now.
I've heard that some with good eyes
can read by moonlight, the faint tracks on the page
like animal whispers but with human meanings.
The light on bare Mediterranean hills
can be like that by day. Whatever moves
has always been there. I know
of no time when a spirit has not been alive
though there can be no proof, only
this longing. That when you are most alone
you are most in love, it is only you can't
touch what it is, hung
above the trees in the light of her
pure being. Whether young or old
it is a time of waiting under thin branches
for the light to clothe itself, the words take leaf.

Postcard

If the bodies had all fallen in one place
there could be a place called
Body, a shrine as it were
to the dead of many wars and other griefs

and the sand would not retreat back to the sea
so the sunbathers and swimmers
could live their lives forever watching each other
from that single place in the world

where the sky's white cotton, wet or dry
is rising and sinking along the rim of an arm
whose pale hairs or dark hairs
stir gently in a breath that could be the wind

the wind coming or going, before or after
the life of that place, and the slow roll of the waves
is a hand turning, pleading, explaining
that this is how it starts, and where it ends.

Soft Voices

Where they came and fed you in time and you
lived on as their child. They are proud
to have done this, but now after each arrest
the posters on your bedroom walls remind them
your name was only provisional, they'd planned
a better one. You are an old man now

though you don't believe it. The world
out there is so bright, the river shining, the trees
shining like water. You are fed by their hands
who took you as their child, only so nervously
you hardly taste a thing. One or two
leave and return from summer vacations and cruises

bringing you back fresh names. At night the soft sands
keep the impression of your skull, the hair thinned
to strands of distant wind. You are our father.
We plant you here to blossom in your own time
between the cat and the dog, above the red ants
and below the katydids. Seven times the quiet earth

will call to you, men drilling through a solid rock
by the streetcar line will pause, just for a moment.
Is there nothing we can do for you, nothing
your seed gathers to ask. Ann, Joan, Henry, Joe
and the old ones who nurtured you so long ago
who are they, and were they wrong?

The Intimacy of Distance

Someone mentioned the *intimacy of distance*
as if we knew what it meant, how
far I have to go to feel
how close you are.
                    But that isn't
what he had in mind. The farther away
the place you long for where you have never been
the deeper inside you it grows
like a human child. But that
was not his point either.
                    To love someone he said
you must be content to imagine her.
But to love in that way
is to circle forever the cold point in the eye
at the centre that sees all things but itself.
                    He could have meant
there is no satisfaction comes to hand
that the hand can keep. It breaks
like a caught bird, soars, returns to the sky
as a mere colour for air.
                    Say blue, say grey.
And yes it vanishes.
And I remember why.

Winter

Strange prophecies often hide
in rainstorms or under puddles.
Flies in the skull of a deer
making the deer sing.

Over the long fields the teeth of fences
whisper to the ants. I never knew
if you were telling the truth.

As poetry spills over its banks
if spoken too long. As the flooded fields
of late January imagine the sun
as an old man a woman's hand.

The dog sleeps her years
in the leaf pile I raked for her bed.
The future breathes so slowly in the old.

Granddaughter

Starting to crawl, she noses to earth
like a mole, it is too hard for her.
She must lie waiting like a seed
until spring when the earth is softer.
No, she is an animal she
can't wait. No says yes and the
arms brace hard and her fingers
dig deeper, the carpet is a field
at night filled with hidden dangers
hunters, shadows, cries. And later
in dreams she will relive this
slow flight through exile, from the
first dark that would claim her again
if it could, straining now
toward the faint horizon of human voices
calling her home, asking her
where have you been, we've waited
a long time, tell us
what it was like back there.

San Michele, Venice

To visit the dead you must cross the water
to an island like this
fringed with black cypresses.

The grand words the long silence
of Ezra Pound has come to this
a simple name without dates

on a stone under a tree so hard to find
it took us more than an hour
the name hidden by leaves
the old name covered with dead leaves.

Back in the place he loved
like Odysseus, back to the island
he loved, who spoke with the dead
in harsh words of blood also

a journey done, almost without companions
in the end. And the living city
behind us sinking slowly west with the sun.

Force and Shadow

The lime after storm light
dulled to olive at the edges of trees
a stillness hung with whispers *place*
I have not taken seriously enough
without wind memory falls
just lies there. One is always

in training and never quite prepared
straining into the silence to hear
another wind, another voice
a red bicycle racing across a blue sea
or from the sky a bird with four black wings
falling, lamenting. So there is

no grief without laughter, my
brave daughters, my mother, father
down the whole line, not hand in hand but
those old pictures. Something passed
hand to hand without hands ever touching
the afternoon rain, the place

momentarily permanent, Neruda's
sad face like a sly gambler's
under a checkered cap, grinning at us.
But it doesn't focus there. The clown
has other business, ways, places to go.
The new moment's movement when it begins
is almost too subtle to catch, the flick
of an eye where force enters shadow
and were you there?

Memo

The way they walked
who were more to you than others
walking towards or away
depending on the mood or time of year

and how close it was
to the beginning or the end
towards or away
anticipation regret

walked with a slight sway
brown tweed skirt blue shoes
toes pointed outward

fine square shoulders set
face tilted up
or down when brooding

someone to meet
coming towards you
someone to regret
leaving turned away

so is the lyric enough
to make memory happen
the day grey or blue
eyes touched with green

and no background? a long
wide street with trees in leaf
the shadow moving behind
asking no questions.

News Fragment

What dies before it is found
known, accomplishes itself.
Simple chemistry. A baby
covered with ants. Found. Alive.

In the morning the rush of cars
bears me with it into the sun.
Moons my mother drank to keep her figure
fertile. Images never lie.

There are dates I felt the abstract waves of fear
pressing on me like a refusal
to understand. Why probe for chaos
with the tip of a pen, your duty

is naming things. Yes but who
can you name, what far witnesses call
to attend your rebirth? Everywhere the grass
is growing faster, thicker –

it is green by day. It is green
also at night, you believe that.
My enigma was always my absence
I heard you say, *I cast no shadow on things*.

O saint, whoever, cry for the one found
alive. Cry for the small ants that have
only to live. Cry for what is forever being
found and is nameless.

Reading Late

What affections I took to be eyes.
Whatever moves the western sky is blue.
Two cars stopping to talk
beside a long green hedge.
The shadows were deepest blue.

The pages turn so slowly.
In later life you discover another
name for the sun
a word much closer to blood.
An irony.

You are here. You were there.
What I loved
were details in an old stone wall.

And the word *edge*
is sharp, not soft. You think
of soft edges, but the words don't meet.
The way her legs swam uphill
in the dry mountain air. And her shoes

like two cars talking
by a long green hedge
until someone yells "Goodbye."

The dark of the western sky.
The western sky is always hungry.
It feeds on the creatures it dreams.
Such ironies I took to be
signs of life.

Illegals

Another killing along the river.
Soap makes the hands clean, a clear
mirror reflects what looks like eyes.

Mother I'm thirsty, said the first child.
Then the necklace broke and her children fell,
scattered. Pity the man with the gun

who has to take care of us. I was
born with legs to run and hands
to ward off evil. To work the dust

into shapes of men and women and sell
for money. A brown-eyed man with a
blue-eyed job he is trained not to hate

saw my reflection and fired. The mothers
wait all their lives for death, so as not
to see death again. But it comes

as a mosquito comes, small, a thin sound.
The brown river runs between our fingers.
The masks we wear to hide us are the sun.

Friday Thirteenth

In the sea the river
drowns. No one has opened this door
for years, the latch has stuck.

Shadowy eyes of dogs
linger in the pitfalls of your dreams.
Who was the woman the woman the one

who wept for you? Crazy garbage
scattered outside, frozen beyond its smell.

Old wooden houses of the old.
Where I imagine I am
they speak no language. The snows

came and went, generations of names
under a roof of sod: into the sunlit
nursery where you felt at peace with light
until the light closed your eyes

and my memory. How old are you now?
I have learned how to form my capitals
and punctuate my sentences. It is

the scream I can't quite control
as the wind can never be silent. Turn

from the beginning to the end
and read it all backward. Ignore
the in-between which is forever where you are.

I have a face for you.
Do you have eyes for me? Eyes
the philosopher said, can only smile in a face
which is the frame of sky where

birds fly. But you began to speak
of the river and the sea. You began
telling me something. Is it where

pain touches us? Give me time
to open your letter and read it.
Somewhere along the trail of sand between words

cities are named, and children. Pauses
where water gathers. Long
winters spent asleep on the smoky ovens
of other ancestries, staying

alive. If a bird flies in
it has lost its way. Keep asking what I meant.

The rain that touched this house.
The roof above it and the stone-grey sky.
All things too simple to know.

Territory

Extravagant under mountains
in the heads of mice
brown mice, grey mice, dogs
axles stuttering through the load of mud

as if borders are what lie beyond the eyes'
peripheries, nowhere more to go, no
start or finish, to wake with nothing in mind
on the rainiest of April Saturdays

at home in the old house
thunder breaking, cold, the dog wanting in
and after a last word with the self who went
his own way years ago and lives up there

in high mountains beyond the rain
in winds beyond the mountains, in such cold
he breaks sticks to make fires, and denies
he was ever my brother

this language that leaves in time
a mothlike dust, a faint powder of lives
fluttering like memory at the womb –
what was it gave the sun so many names

and in the intellect a flame still as glass
hard as this pebble I found.

Gernika

All night a thin *g*
on a distant string...

The revolution must begin
in our hearts.

We who know how to use time
will prevent it

this time. O Mother
who stole your milk from us.

Madrid, May 2001

Winter Grass on the Plains

The beach where whoever's footprints made it in
was it Amelia or some castaway, they
found so little. At that edge
where life is always beginning, starting over
as if it had never happened: a ship's
broken wheel or the long wheel of a wagon
missing one spoke – into that gap crawls
an idea like a legend. Where spread is so wide
that nothing is tall enough to be vertical
then who can find you. I miss
myself. I miss the memory of you there
in the other room, in the far part of the house
that keeps its own night and day, its
weather, hours, directions. Out there
on the rim of the sea, at the edge of the cattle pond
the silvery grass shines under low dark cloud
and this is what the searchers found when they came
expecting nothing they could call their own.

Late Night Movie

What air can you collect that you won't
match me grain for grain to say my prayers
a window, say, the long sparse light
opposite for hundreds of miles, a land
rolling and characterless except for the TV screen
where a man and a woman shape their love
to fit the pattern we are willing to bear
as extras, all of us. I have in mind
a spirit that won't refuse, being foolish, to run
the beautiful eyes of the visionary or saint
whose cold shadow walks past him
counting all his moments without a name
under the long sun: to prepare his place
in the absence of any party further to this
which is anywhere anywhere now
you name the place we'll build the town around it
this is the man this is the woman. These ones.

Wild Eyes

I have set plaster to catch a foot.
Who is the runner who passes every day
              leaving nothing behind him.

As the rains begin
autumn is still a ghost
or an unborn child waiting to name its mother.

Headaches and the rain!
In mourning for his dog the poet wrote
              dog a thousand times.

At three in the morning the sun is too close.
How can I organize the events
that led me here.

            Where

is the money. What time did the train leave
bearing away my sins
the memory of my father ending with me.

Frictions

A man running on a background of wind
among graves. Where is the suit
on the empty hanger. How long
can I play.

The picture of a heart done in blue crayon
on white paper. Somewhere
they exchanged eyes.

A man running in an unlucky direction
calling out to someone. The light is against him.

The light is in his eyes
as the trees turn the leaves burn.

As the leaves fall *fric fric*
on the dry pavement. How far can he run
calling calling against the hurt light
his hands reversed
his head and feet

reversed. The coat hanger and the man
are both naked. Something

fell on the roof. Something
falls on the roof
where the house stood.

This is a painting about a change of season
a change of heart affecting the mind of light.

So little time to notice little things.

How the Elderly Are Born

I heard them speak of the *elegance of rain*
in the brown slum garden. The old
had wooden hands. They clicked their fingers
and I caught the soft voice of Lupe Salcedo:
"I have no animosity towards my lovers
only hate." And the shutter fell
and cut them off at the neck. Though
they had done nothing wrong but wandered
into the wrong frame, like inadmissible memories
that won't let go, evidence of lost time
or time one must face among strangers. No one
knows me here. I take my life in my hands
that open and close like an overdue book
of hours so personal there are no signs.

Sunlight Through Blinds, Four O'clock, Facing West

Whoever comes stepping through the frame
make it worthwhile for us now.
Beyond the trees there is a river
and beyond that a dark headland
knifed by the prow of a long canoe
forever still in its movement.
And my eyes fail, and give back
whatever it was they saw
whatever it was they understood they saw
for it is blank now. I go to live
in some future of memory among
the howls of the skins of dead animals
who spread their soft-eyed bones
over mountains and plains and through towns
where the light picks us up and walks us home.

Bethlehem

The late-night light that accompanies
the companionless, the white
neon light no one can turn off
god knows how many miles between towns
as quiet as this one.
                      When the child is born
it will have visitors. The first to come
they shall be holy.
                      What did she think
when they asked her name and her husband's
business there, whispering to themselves
until daylight put out the light.
What do they dream in the dark
when the wind brings a baby in its mouth.

Incarnations

Every fart begins
as a breath of fresh air

A dry old man
who talks to himself
and to animals

He would twist the sun if he could
Wring it out
Eat it as bread. Eat

Corn Woman said. But
If you forget to think of me
or make use of me
without remembering my words

And Dawn the tawny one
doe bloodied by the arrow that pierced
her father in their lovemaking

Her sadness will spread too
to the other animals

To write my empty page
in this book that others have written

As a bird watches
another eating
a berry

Eyes eyes everywhere always
No way out of it

Three dogs tossing a cat
until it is only a skin filled with blood
Watch and do nothing

*In the beginning
is always something
that later gets hidden*

The burden of a poem is its own
lightness. Who can hear
me

Rustle of ants carrying leaf-bits
to their nest at the earth's centre
Eyes of danger

To write and fill my page
with emptiness

Though nature compensates
A man born without eyes
might have two assholes

Dry old man
Dry twigs rubbed together
Happiness that is born
not of desire

*He is the shadow that precedes
the body*

comes and goes

*as fire goes home
withdraws to its dark house*

Silence
is a part of speech

You kneel
And then you are free.

It Happens

A house's perfect time is when
the frame is up, not yet the roof and siding.
The young wood is still warm to the touch.
You feel the grace and tension of the bones.

Later there will be shadows. Lives
clothed in lives. Rooms filled
and rooms to spare, the crying aloud
of love and birth and death. Young wood grown old.

I have made this happen too fast
too suddenly. In between is where things gather
to wear their masks and dance their winter spring

with a fine sense of occasion. Time
is forever on our side. Who would believe
the face in the old hall glass still bears your name.

Watermarks

    I

The dog trots up to sniff the tree
The dog trots back again

The dog trots up to sniff the tree
The dog trots back again

The dog trots up to sniff the tree
The dog trots back again

The tree waits

    II

Blue waits in you
as a dream waited behind the sun.

American man
is a son of a gun.

The wheat field weaves
spiders who are thin men.

III

A man turns round and round
on the street corner. Something
he can't find or is trying to
complete, in himself
or around himself. His feet

own nothing but
the circles he makes. The deep
city around him siphons off noise
like a time-funnel. Earth

is extra. Earth is a
ring of bones. When in time I'm asked
to greet the stranger whose suit is worn
from mere rain and the sun. He
does not resemble my father, or yours.

Apples and Apples

When she was a girl in Palestine
a soldier made her promises.

The wind off the sea
was a hand caressing her back –

inland the windblown sand
bit deep as bone.

I came upon her early.
She came upon me late.

Or put it another way, she had
lived more, longer, passionately afraid

where I was timid. Seven years between us.
Seven planets, seven stones smeared with blood.

We were both wanderers. But
she'd had to learn to live in ways

where I was innocent, death
in Europe had been real. For her

the subterfuge of languages.
For me the words we shared.

Too early and too late
can't average out as just in time.

Apples and apples. A door open
is always just closing.

No joy there now, no grief.
Fierce numbers feed the stars.

Nocturne

House like a restless sleeper
shifts here
            settles there
suddenly
doors don't fit

Mother swift feeding her young
drops too far down the chimney
            out the flue
flits from room to room
            wall window door
fighting the dark
a fact
brushing a dream

Awake now
now not
image of arctic sun
            all night
around the eye's horizon
circling

            animal
gentle or fierce
pure wonder
            in this house
fitted to my bones

Through trees the follow-through
of night wind asking birds
            hello the screech owl calls
closer to time

far wheels driving hard
around dangerous curves
         the old road
      even at this hour
who's coming home

Father why are you
waiting for me
         your train left
almost thirty years ago
on rails of fire
        in winter
ashes to earth
where mother went first

Tomorrow a blank page
tonight a poem
the furnace where seeds of words
         melt and cry
wanting lives
wanting mouths

to kiss
to speak
      I breathe
grateful to hear the birds.

Call Notes

I looked over the long valley
before I started down
acres and acres of other people's
strangeness —
roofs, cars, a barn, children running —

what time was it
the colours I wanted to touch
this angle, that flatness

like coming home, but
the smell of others' cleanliness
a faint cry from the white house
a name just a sound —

there, there, running —
a girl's dress red as poppies
catching the sun

the long valley a face facing a face
facing it
in sudden time

the windy place you come to —

Impression

Quiet, and the hill settles
toward light, makes
this less difficult.

In the dark you were a figure of dream
eyes come gone a figure of laughter
mocking us. The clock
we fear is only our own waking

as the numbers rise.
Days nights sun and moon
the numbers. The clock
is my mouth.

Overland they come in wagons
making no noise. Their names
are a long paper sheet of wind

and if I am their son or was their father
you are what else to me? The rocks
never spoke. The water
rose up high then fell and dried to powder.

I have done these things well
those things badly.
You come to me now asking for more.

*As long as the grass shall grow
or the waters run* they promised.
The skull I found is abuzz with memories
or words that are memories

as if the fears I took to be yours
were mine all along. Curved
like seashells or old swords
or bamboo in the rain, bent

to earth like a sheltering mother.
In the dark when you came you were
a light. But the coming of light

killed you. Light
which is everywhere but not at once, your
face changes, your eyes soften, harden, die.

One of us is wrong.
Who. The other. Now
daybreak, now noon. Who
gave us these names.

Lucky Numbers

      I

I dream sometimes
we meet
and there is regret
that after all
the chances
there was no chance.

But trouble
in someone's life
after which
the sand keeps falling

and the sun
seen through smoky glass

                        only unnerves the dark
                        does not detain it

long. White against black
in formal squares along a winter path.
White air. Crack of thunder or bone.

      II

Where nothing walks are shadows
of other things. Trees. A broken fence.
A pot of flowers. That tank
hidden under branches of veins.

What do I know which year.
A hand of cards, fanned, held close.

A wine-stained wooden table
the rain raining outside

months of patient waiting
someone's child by the hand.

III

Who are the refugees?
Where have they hidden their eyes?

Your uncle has a weak fart.
He will die.

Then let the wind
carry his whisper off
to the ant queen's nest

before winter comes –

I bear no man a grudge.
I speak because I'm spoken to.
When my smell dies
another smell revives
to take its place.

Blue, yellow, red
what flower are you?

Of Magic

Because she was always dusty and dirty, they called her Cinderella. Light of my tired eye. Who was a father left thus where the light fell dead. Or music emptied of sound, just a tremor, like a far-off eye watching unseen. When the prince came he had a bad limp. Things change, there is nothing to be said that hasn't already been described, over and over again, in the way words have of startling into life like a herd of grazing deer panicked by someone's footstep. Has he come? Yes, but that is not the one I dreamt would come. Hand me the broom. Tonight is overtime.

Not There Yet, Nowhere Near

Morning. Across the hills
cistercian rain, a thousand-year-old
silence.
                Eyes (Wittgenstein)
can only smile
in a face. What you would be or do
after it ends.

When it said its voice I said no this is
arithmetic, stop counting.
Silence. Music. Give me time to go
where the light is.

Red, yellow, blue
the cardinal colours.
Three the perfect number. No
fish, flesh or eggs.

Great Horned Owl and I are awake
his eight-syllable call
with a pause in the middle
                the downward glide
on the last note
like a child's complaint. I'm hungry.

Morning a grey feather.
Moderation of rain, whisper of
old prayer. Cultivated hunger
in the gardens of wind.

                And the news.
Police searched the school.
A robot blew up a backpack.
Nothing was found.

Lifelines

Placenta
abandoned on an anthill.
Lives I have left.

To feed with my hands
my mouth, your body
my blood, finger by
finger loosening.

Lives I have left
behind. Red and brown
the paired cardinals
sing into the tempo of the sun

– mistakes my hands make
choosing words. Future
loosens like soil around an old root.

And I have avoided your graves
as well as I could,
the precise hour or place
my obligation.

The burnt photos and the letters gone
are like old hunger, eaten alive.
When someone asks my name I give your names.

Late May, black pieces of sun
circle on wings overhead.
The smell of spring earth

is perfect. Mother
you come to me always as rain.
I have had no victories.

The other dead
will not go away.
No one will let them
go, I live in silence.

In knowledge, in ignorance.
What can I say will be heard.
We who parted company

so long ago knew only
what we were. The curse
of poetry is this desire for beauty
where none survives. Only

questions, ashes. There are
no favourite poems. Dead spiderlegs,
a dried moth by the window, time.

I burn you now
and in burning you
myself. The mouths of ants
cut cleanly as fire.

High Winds and Heavy Snows

When you look up
from your book
so suddenly –

having remembered nothing
of the last ten pages

but your absence of mind –
the words were strangers
in a foreign city, one

familiar to you only in dreams
where a voiceless thought tells you
this is *here, that* is where you are

and each native like each snowflake has a face
and the wind they speak is untranslatable –

a look in your eyes so lost
you could be anywhere at any time –

and I hide my face
not wanting to be found.

Memo

Who does not want my child
may not have her

the long tongue of thirty years
I find dry pavement
here is the word you sing

like sunlight indefinite
to be trusted not loved
to be loved but not trusted

like ancient rain
to be drunk by small degrees
as dry words

and where have they buried us
who put the squirrels to dig here
looking for names

these are particulars
there is no ledger only the sound of wind

oleander in a valley in Spain
below the broken goat corral
much later

mother daughter together
think together think
of time as like the feathers of a bird

clutching what can't be kept
the air his eyes
looking elsewhere away

here are words for you
that stone won't take
they are not strong enough

there is no apt photograph
no faithful likeness

now you are free to live.

The Colour of Rocks, of Bread

can live where there are stories
blue in the depth of a pail
someone's old paint

A human face
always appears to be waiting
some sudden knowledge

and the desert appears to be shallow
because there are few shadows
Where light is everywhere
who touches what

And can a finger claim
it has that experience
I was there I felt you move

If that season could return
always appears to be waiting
the certainty there's nothing more
a hand can say

a hand burnt onto cement
a human profile photographed
on white rock

ancholia the columbine
flower of sadness some
of madness others

But the best bread talks to you
You live it as you eat it
a messenger thirsting for breath
at the end of his hot race
against time

        heat/cold

muscat grapes
laid out to dry as raisins in the sun
the few dry facts that stand between
a life or a death sentence

As the desert is finally home
It is your shadow I fail to see
so far away so bright my eyes fail.

Answers

What is the time of day
listening in a stone
warmed in an old woman's hand
on a concrete bench
in a square in an old town

a name older than mine
though grass drifts in the air
at the same instant I hear
the wind blow her skirt from black to shadow
like weather changing

when we return from war
when they returned from wars
the garden was always there waiting
though the postcards have turned brown
a dog's jaw buried to help

corn or alfalfa grow
a superhighway crosses the bridge
that connects time as it joins
both shores that long ago were one
was it her dog her garden

her son who didn't return
is she Dolores or Maria
or Kristen Helen Angelique
waiting for the sun to marry the wind
like weather turning

a name older than the town
an older name than any town
the square the fountain named for who
first put it there
no clock heard anywhere

to what lover she gave birth
who drank her wine and left her dry
the wind to blow it all away
as footsteps up the rocky path
the stone drops from my hand.

Master of Wind

I was not quick enough
or too quick, and you hadn't moved.

Into my hands fell the old air
of paint on canvas, indoor words
settling like flies.

One century then another
stirred the calendar. My hands

opened and closed. *I am
so sorry I can't be there
our lives take time* –

memory split in half
like silence in old wood –

cries, thrown on the flame.
And you hear your birth over and over again
in the spring grass.

One of us here.
One of us there.

Vanished Numbers

The shops are closed
        light finds other shadows

in that face
a crooked sign
        a night lit with rain

that memory is all breath can spare
for imagining   one sign or two
to open

virtualities
a hand banging metal   is it Cain
the blacksmith
        no stranger now

marked by fire

One goes   then two   ten
that the race survive   or that it die

night wet with such light
no name   no place   no tokens
the rain a kind of dignity
        thin wash of milk

into whatever's face lifts gazing up
with no reason to count or hope

City   City of ours
O night of
        hidden answers
                vanished numbers

leaf   arrow   vein.

Seed Light

Singularly where the sky walks
the flight of a bird
         hand-me-down
to wrestle with nothing
is to have no strength

but the wind is not nothing
you can avoid
         though not know
backwash of intellect
moving the river
         to and fro
the way coitus might happen

I would like to begin
    I would have liked to begin
owning nothing
but my beginning

not star nor telescope
walking the light of my seed
     up, into the infinities of touch

in the cold air
no angel
given my name.

Fugitives

A man turning his back
shot while attempting to escape
white peasant cotton, wide hat.

Why this dream now
while the light bends slowly up through the trees
on panther feet. I must
organize. Age is like the light

crossing slowly. In there are bodies
I never knew, eyes, fingernails,
an amplitude of names caressing themselves

desiring others. The man
falls, and there are holes of blood
spreading over the continent. Nothing
cries in the early heat where dust is cover.

That was long ago. Though dreams
welcome men who would escape, and the women
who come to understand, who always

understood. I keep my word; I hide
him and feed him, blot his wounds.
I open my eyes now watching

the trees bend in the wind, while over the grass
on hands and knees come shadows
and syllables of light, the young
helping the old along until they become air.

Man Carrying a Suitcase

There is a time
under the river
fish swim with such grace

a shadow to catch
a shadow disembarking from
an escalator of wind

crying someone's name
in time to catch the taxi
of his life –

alone as the body
always is itself
resembling no one

though names come to mind
names like numbers
running on two legs

in someone's mind –
the catastrophe of keeping
up with things

across the floor
out through the portal of light
between this shore and that

a flash of anonymous love
someone not important
where do they go.

Eyes

The last buddha was lost
in one of our moves

what you don't look after
someone takes
so life changes, and lives change

and in the end do you care
what you have and are
so many things wander out there
nameless as snow or rain

hands looking to reach
anything more solid than mere touch
a word, a parable

her profile on a transatlantic ship
looking out to sea, which is nowhere
what remains when the eyes go
eyes, that is, of memory

the accuser and pardoner
the one you can never trust
but call your father

dry old man who must go
and you must follow

not quite, because her face
is never the same
her womb an acorn or a maple seed
or a garden where deer walk

step by step
like a thing coming to mind
a memory, or its forfeiting

to desire, a different opening
or ending, mice
lost in the sun, field mice
alive under the snow

her profile becoming eyes
that look at you
another year when the sea
that year when the sea

on blank days
they look down from windows
as if watching for you to come home

but you have moved so often
you could be anyone.

Departures

They hung
stations from her eyelids
with real trains –
Anna, or
whoever takes her place.

Across the wind-darkened harbour water
white sails. Mud and rain
tracked in on children's feet.
Where, where have you been?

The lonesome train of her heavy century
long gone. Explosions still to come.
For me, a silence
in my ears, a winter
haiku –

*Shimogyō ya
yuki tsumu ue no
yoru no ame*

> *In the lower town
> across the heaped-up snow,
> whisper of night rain*

One is so frail.
Two are hardly better.
They were jackhammering the street outside
a day before the news came.

I like to think the snow
will give her back her shadow.
Milk across darkening grass, the cold.
Daphne gone to tree,
doe-ears flicking.

Histories

It was another country
and none of us understood
the mission of the conquerors
was to lose themselves

lose themselves, and find
what someone else had named
before they came
in words they could never pronounce
sounds muffled to the tongue

like bones, woman bones
had yours not burnt to ash
words muffled to the tongue
father mother love

such fierce life this new world
they came to enslaved
by their age-blackened sun
dream of a golden wilderness

your missing letters to me
my ones to you I burnt
to an ash whiter than bones
because the voice I found there
was that of a frightened child

mine, but not mine. Now this
memory of our lives
and how the conquest took us
takers, taken, one by one.

Were we a people a place
or was the hair teeth eyes
made into masks, given names
the painted masks of clowns

who live in comedies how people
come to grief, rise
and grace us with tears and words
a history that won't end

no jesus no nails of blood
no mission no cross no
blessed name of mary
to see us through

the deceit of poetry
the astonishment of a death without
angels the long still lines
who wait under theater marquees
silent in the cold spring rain.

Wind

There's a loud word for it
and a soft word. It is not

everywhere, but somewheres
and while it is there

is everything. Deep song
the thumb strums

can fill the heart. Let
this anger between us end –

a mirror can wake the sun
like nothing on earth.

We are blessings all of us.
We scatter like air.

New Year

First day, writing into the grey
morning silence
                as through falling snow
my daughters my son.

He said, I have stories to tell you.
If the words taste bitter they're mine.

But it is another year. The wind
opens leafless mouths in the trees
not song but wind.
                Shan Silver Ana Matt
such distances those Indian ponies crossed
riding away, their backs turned
to ourselves who are not there.

Who are you where are you going?
Hard to hold you still
bring you close.

A story that asks for help
as in the African picture-word
I lift you from the river
with my hands
                But I say no

I'm not the one
you think, the story-man
try there, try
the internet, look there
where must be helpful hands.

I light my fire for you
with paper words. Winter is cold.
In January oak leaves still fall
on the north wind, old
boyhood omen, friend.

Come play. Come play
as what struggles there
in the deepening snowflake.

You had a friend and a time.

Grey to pale half-white as the sky
red dots in the distance meaning
a name forming

a body coming home.

Cat and Mouse

What does a poem want?
Huts without doors
and blind children peering.

More than a measure of rain.
Air that blows in and out of lives
promising, threatening. To
close the door on eyes that have no language

like a wandering comma
in a line of words. Who
witnessed my birth, or yours, that
what isn't fair might be acceptable

at last. So somewhere
something gives, breaks.
I am my own understood.

In the woods below the house vultures settle
in the winter-bare elm tops
(how many, why there)
is a story waiting, some tale

with a sun and a moon
and whatever stars the universe can lend
to outwait this winter. A woman
who knew she must die, but would risk that

because. Whose birth
was irreplaceable. What have you done
to identify the question in your mind

like a lathe turning, like metal wailing.
Cat's eyes watch me from the deck outside
her coat fluffed for the cold. Always
one imagines wind

in the stillest of air. Soft feet
padding along the sky
children of thunder. And would the truth

truly be interesting?
Whose habit do you break
when you break silence?
What must be said for whose sake –

like naming a stone
then throwing it away.
"Old friend…" the letter begins
or might have.

A poem watches with big eyes
like children startled in a doorless yard
no grass just dust. As if

silence ever was. I am
the record of something never said, it says.
Watch as the light turns my way.
It is the mask of the sun.

Lights Across the Lake

Who's memorable is what water answers
reflectively, the first date

that failed for want of experience
as must have happened in that scented garden

where fruit hung heavy and fell.

Nothing survives stupidity.

One summer at a time goes dark.
The vigil of old eyes

turns on itself. No reason to mourn
what was never there, a touch

that began and ended at the
same moment. Except now looking across

the darkened lake of fifty years
something naked swims close, with her eyes

a wavelet
breaks at my feet.

Scattering

Brother and sister
the light turns their way.

Outside, sun covers the snow.
No time. No wind.

In the light
they look thin.

❧

Distress is what focuses the eyes.
Something, a
disturbance, panic, angels.

The last time I was home
it wasn't there.

❧

You are half the time what I'm not ever.
Where it went wrong
enough for us to see.

The holy ghost is, what, an ancestor.
God help that in our hands.

My shadow moves
slowly across the clockface
like a third eye.

No, the third eye's finger
probing every place
the circle wants to stop.

    ❧

Ouch for chrissakes that was my head.
Give me time with your ghost.

I am only
inches ahead of you. Give me

your hand. One or
other of us will be born

tonight.

    ❧

Tomorrow
becomes today. Two
figures backlit by a rising moon

are turned which way
the light
or the risen dark.

Struggling to be reasonable.
The cold helps.

What I turn into

unmasks I am

with no bitterness.

❧

You were passionate once
and called things by their names
listening for the echo
of your name. Whoever
did this needs to know that.

❧

I step on my shadow
searching for yours. The lost

penny I pick up
brings the thought of luck, it

might have been yours, or if
the stranger cared. One

loses what another finds.

❧

I imagine the Cross
as a garden filled with wind.

Two people meet there, calling to a third
who never comes.

Light falls evenly on all the stones.

What matters is to see the picture form.

No otherwise.

Time Out

Out there, rain telling the trees
to repeat their leaves

Father, you are the shadow
I stepped from

You I haven't talked to for years
bear with me

Out there, the rain
saying nothing but rain

saying this.

Gathering

My brother came to me
asking for water.
I said, this is Mother's glass
it is empty now.
He drank, and I drank.
My breath remains.

❧

How can I speak of giving.
Leafy spring comes out
to tease us into trusting it.
Another life, it says, another
life. When the killing ends
in Ramallah – but whose
hands can lift the dead
with the absolution of stones.

❧

We talked of nothing else
but how hungry we were.
Like cattle with noses forever
to the grass, bent that way
at sunset. Not one looked up
to see the sky we saw.
But their heaven was green.
Their eyes were home.

❧

The young painters,
young in their colours.

Had we been
bewildered then? Walking
10,000 invisible steps later
the reds of inflamed eyes
green of a rainy afternoon
in the almost empty gallery
darkening the years back
to where they started from.

∂℞

"You are too serious."
Then let's forget I said that.
"Oh no, just say it again
with a smile."
I smiled and said it again.
And saw it was a lie.

∂℞

A father goes without saying.
A mother would like to fill all
the silences with that look she has.
Time can remember
only what the children say.
Look, learn silence from their eyes.

∂℞

My brother came to me
asking for water.
I said, this is Father's glass
it is empty now.
He drank, and I drank.
My breath remains.

Vegetation

I

Was awakened by my body uttering
strange syllables; a conspiracy of ants
or politicos from some terror making plans
that concerned us all. I'd dreamed
of my children, of cats pretending to be
my wives, and the air had a smell
of ancestries beyond my memory.
Then the sun opened the room
and some name kept telling me its child
whose cries were redbirds in the cedars.
These are the messengers you live with
by day, and become, at night, if lucky
your old self. I can never remember
why I say *myself* reluctantly.

II

The great hackberry
at the top of the drive
half dead, half green
comes into spring now
like an old woman
whose memory is gone
where green lives bud again
from the living half
whose dead half clings to it
having nowhere to go
keeping the form of the tree's
whole grace intact, sun, rain

the same messenger now
no telling how or when.

III

Rain, rain again. If
I were grass I'd be happy.
Where memory rests… The slow
trickle of water, long
husbanding undertow that keeps sanity
fresh. Nothing to hide from.
All that is is here
the voice says, what you fear
has already happened. Wait
until the rain makes eyes
that look at you directly.
There are no honest mirrors.
I say *eyes, eyes* as though
the eyes were my own.

Spring 2001

Where was there what time
Is where we begin…
Collect again what scattered

come, go, came, went
an order of verbs
too close to the fingertips
slips out is gone

fragment of a Mediterranean coastline
with blue-white villas   on sand
behind the closed concession stand
a pair of shoes
left waiting   it's no go

out of humour
out of touch

and comes the spring wind
a time for booking journeys
making time
walk ahead on its own feet

warm-green smell soft wind
confusion of waking dreams
lost in some city   gone
if our voices weren't
angry   time

bad and good
in whichever order
my sister, we

survivors, old ones now
ourselves

we, us
taught her 35-year-old parrot
to sing the 'Ave Maria' along with her
the sweet and raw voice

mingling   confused in the sun
where was there
that time

March-month   I was your son
I know your wind
that strip of gentle coast where others
always lived   paper, sand

the scattered pieces
I collect
myself.

Book Closing

The last guests fetch their coats
and walk off home. Turning autumn
their shadows enter night.

Lights on the steep hill far left.
Whiff of coal, tobacco smoke.
Words thinning to air, air dies.

Did you learn why they couldn't see you
thinking you invisible like
the dead in their graves? Were they

the first friends, who lived until sunrise
and opened life and death for you
like an old book, a stream of numbers

voices, riffling on, beyond? *He will grow
tired of me,* she said. *Sleep,* and went
silent. The page writes itself.

Now they are all gone.
Scorpion, bull, lion. And
the little one, a pisces, like these hands.

Solo with Grazing Deer

Mother's son, father's son.
Late spring, the rain hangs on
like lost sleep.

A smell of fresh soap
when the wind drops. In the field below
a horse neighs. The wet cedars

bend to earth, looking for their roots.
Waxwings tilt and soften
the grey air between branches.

Memories still to come
like waves that haven't yet happened
gazing out across the wall of sea

to where the sea ends. The deer
gone. Myself I've been saying goodbye to
all my life. Beads of rain

like a series of clear names
run together. One, then a
thousand. Then the whole sea boiling.

The Naming of Absence

When I drip ink on a white page
it is morning. Wet or dry
are the shadows around eyes
that walk slowly toward the past

looking for the signs that filled with water
something lost and always something found
a button or a broken comb
not that. You are unlovable

says the grammar of fingers
tapping out the keys the wind dictates
like notes of a song. The
voice of an adjective, the noun's face

streaming in the muted lights of rain –
what is meaning – I can tell you
I was there, as I am here, and the light talks to me
in the voice of an injured animal

accusing the night of being dark
the day not sufficient to heal her.
Where are you going with your hands raised like that?
The day barely begun, and there are cries

happy cries
from the village square. Dreams
that condemned the night to the darkest of blues
drain from the hand basin and leave me

empty of thoughts. The naming
of absence begins in the need to love
what can't be touched: as that
in the middle distance, memory of someone

stripped or clothed, in a field between two trees
is looking away across a distant fence
of calling, or silent. Beyond the subdivision
dies the prairie. I'm inclined to wonder

why I waited so long and no one, nothing –
leaves are falling. What is memorable
must have lived one time, along
the edge of a river or a line of railings

painted fresh black. One hand can touch
so much emptiness. You came away
one afternoon on the late train south
and we crossed the strait and spent two days and nights

at an old hotel, understanding
the time was ours. I think of my childhood
all the years since as being these days
coming as they did to warn us of mornings

later, without eyes. I've given
each of my fingers a secret name, its own
name and memory. The pages of the book
keep turning, and so many are empty.

ASTERISKS

2007

For Guit, who is here

To row through the silence

TOMAS TRANSTRÖMER

*The most beautiful is the object
which does not exist*

ZBIGNIEW HERBERT

*

1.

Shredded pulp, glue
of history,
    page upon page
pressed flat. In every word
in and between each cry

a body, a some
one, not
clothed or naked or named

Let the sun
attend to this,
fingers of concrete
feet spared the grass

Cut us doors less tall
so we may enter on our knees

Look down   Look down.

*

    2.

They're digging the field
that took them in
from exile in the sand

The man bent double can see
where a woman
lay down with her child

Ant, she sings
come home
to where
distress has no other smell

now, ever.

*

    3.

Two branches
Two birds
    one eating
    one watching

if one were to fly off
the other would have no purpose

More to
where you are
than
here I am.

*

    4.

Legs   legs
little girl springs
    up and down
apart from where
the wind goes, a part

of the wind
who is a junkie with a clear head
a capsized star
in its youngest sex

Has her own name
jumps higher and higher
to reach to touch it.

*

    5.

The lifesnake uncoils
into that hole
where water
is driest   On a billboard

a woman is swimming
away, toward sunset
  and life returns
    where you were

rain silences by touch
the apple of thought.

*

    6.

When the blade falls
between seasons too slow to notice
or fear and happiness
    tongue in a dry mouth
avid to taste again

All images spent
in the long search for one
    that needs nothing more
than a brave sunset on a blue sea

to settle upon like a white bird
at rest on the endlessness of an expanding wave

no street address
the same
as any other.

*

7.

Is there life after
poetry?   All that the
past caught   would
perhaps,
return to itself –
       mind gone back
now, to life's proper calling,
life.

Some things will dance
and others will lie still.

If we detect a singing
it is theirs.

*

     8.

    quick strokes of the pen
marking time.   Not sounds
but shapes for sounds

Where can I hide
asked the child

By noon
windabsent. Clouds
wet or dry, climb
     hand over hand
the day's heat

Where, asked the child
is my selfshape, place to hide

a sound
within a sound

a breathing in, not out.

*

  9.

This mark refers you to
another place
  fire, her star
an unpronounceable name
whose wherebeing
  kept old light

She had a way with her
What lovers saw
  or missed
in her eyes
was an ancient event
a murdered light
  gone black

Texture of an empty chair

vacated air.

*

    10.

Winter makes better poems
better moons

Name
no mere name
no name
    merely name

quanta, light
up there
where things fall

Sing
birds of dawn

the unidentifiable
that is always there

Light
pitting a tin roof
like rain.

*

11.

Dreams: radical doors
forever open, closed

Wake at night to the crying of a spotted fawn
taken by something –

unknown yet familiar
city of strangers
all on first-name terms
        whose meanings are forbidden

Here there has been a death
or a vanishment –
self, cold-case detective
in search of his shadow

        too late, as often
among the clueless footprints
leading here or there

choose whichever.

*

    12.

We come home in the sense
there is that,
waiting or gone.

        A deep
vowel draws us. Otherwise
what lurks in pastures
or lingers in dark city streets

is air that touches
nothing.

      An old sandal
its mate lost
is home. The air
in an emptied pen.

Not examples, images.

Memory of a loving hand
stroking
what night
makes afraid.

*

13.

Spotted fawn is back.
Then what was that cry the other night?

No, there were three.
Lucky or unlucky three.

Both eyes
and the eye between,
the hidden bead of wisdom.

Sincerity of milk.

Duck between mother's legs
and life will flow.

Deer crowd the little lawn.
Rush-hour as I scatter food.

One hand, a dozen mouths.
The furred air we breathe.

*

    14.

True form
    of no-form

It is after and before
memory

I separate
water from water
    with my hands

What is there
was predictable, but
who would have guessed
    it is this

air the live-oak fills.

*

15.

Every poem, however
obscure, is a revealment

Before this
there was nothing

Air
costs so much,
breath, lives

The desert's dead children
continue to grow,
grow beyond the lives
they might have uttered

Silence though is heroic
Silence is
the future that precedes

breath.

*

16.

When a man and woman
separate
the children follow
where they can —

The wind outside the door
opens its arms,
and what was a breath across
face, hair

becomes a body
without a name
with open arms.

No one leaves entirely.

Look around you and see
which side your shadow falls —

Spin round, spin round
to catch it as it falls.

*

17.

They scattered the fires
and rode on.
   A few bones
catch the wind and drift off as ash.

What talk costs...

In the future are settlements.
Now
dusty soldiers go elsewhere
and breed new freedoms.

   Have a good day.

We in turn
sleep less
and make it count.

*

    18.

What have you done to yourself?

The fruits you loved to eat
    peel and eat
slice gently open to make
    perfect tongue-tip bites

in season
each in season –
everything and everyone
in season –

Life always replenished itself
always
    fruits in season –

Until

no pit
  no seed
    no stone

your hands went empty.

*

19.

The knife-cut knuckle
almost hides its scar,
    my singular addiction
to old wounds.

In the village street
a drunk fell
and crawled away
up steepness into darkness.

Dry summer, dry year.

Then that night, a sprinkle
"Rain', spat José,
"I call that bird-piss"

The pictures faded now.

Old olive sacks
the memories
ripped and tossed aside.

*

20.

After so long heat
mindbone picked clean

Burnt in the light
between halves –

    one eye
    another eye

Is the rain
    fire's enemy
merciful to fire

or does the occasion matter
the time of mind
    between darknesses

To love
To be of use.

*

21.

Du Fu: "How will poems
bring honour?"

I cut at this –
So that we talk about –

beauty of
fine language.

The soldiers of dust
want to come home now.
Blood mixed with dust

is metaphor.

As dying is like
nothing.
      Help me ask

a question that has no answer.
A poem nothing can read

but itself.

*

    22.

Light, colourless
as numbers are colourless
as memory
       loses
vividness

As memory acquires grief
and grief's opposite
    grieflessness
wit in the playing down of things

In the dry leaves
a child falls dead
gets up again
      gets up
and the game goes on
against the play of bare walls

Lights off   Lights on
the sun unlocks its world

The sun
remembers to.

*

23.

October, the hands spread
then fall away

At the mind's edge
distant sound of bombing
             only the wind,
deafening light.

Clarity of skies above history
in a child's picturebook –

Who talks to begin a sentence
end a thought
             before words
turn cold –

Soul of a sparrow
pecks at bread
beneath a café table –

It's time to go, move on
as you said once, and did.

*

24.

Village, hills, blue sea

You look for something
that isn't there,
so you invent the thing
you're looking for –

Wheat, olives, vines, figs
the plains for progress
the hills for mere survival

Same crop at different altitudes,
different harvest months
but the same prayers –

Earth, heart,
opens so very slowly

rain, wind, sun
and the swallows come and gone
each one nameless.

*

25.

There comes a point
where large and small
    are identical –

an eye
and everything it sees
    encompassed in one glance –

Some line is now being crossed
that stays in place
    until it is time again

to resume, retrace
if only, now, as a shadow
    the lengthening spiral of words

that ancient path between fields

that brought us here.

*

   26.

Twitchtail squirrel
headdown down the tree
for water, comes –

quick neighbour of mine
eats, drinks, at the cat's bowl
when the cat's not there

Drought all winter now
fires across the high plains
    the rain is angry
New Year's come and gone

Another stick from my fire
waits to light itself
with whatever breath I save

Old man Old wind

squirreltails.

*

27.

One by one they go
    the old languages
        the little tongues

Birdwings heard at daybreak
they enter and leave
the back way –

There there
old ones
    old songs
        old bones of songs.

*

28.

Syllables, buried like nuts
at half-forgotten points
in the strawdry winter grass.

What don't wake
don't sleep.

Once or twice
in an old love letter
the words come back, to say
close to a one that spoke once

where have you gone.

*

29.

Sunburst, August '45
city gone
       wasted eyes

through the fire
darkly gone. To hide
is to be forever at large –

burned on memory
       on white stone
eyes that crowd my darkness –

Eyes who lived
who found the sun

Nothing, nothing to be done.

*

30.

Grass inflames the sky
Grass and the inarticulate gifts of grass
go up, up.

Smoke is a verb.
Wind is a verb.
Grass is a noun, like stone.

Words burn away words.

Set a dish of poetry under a tree.
A bird will find it, some creature.

Oh, it cries.
what now   what now.

*

31.

The old painter
took the colour ochre
scraped away at the mountain
to the mountain's bones

Under the hot dry sun
the broad hat
    his fierce eye thinking

In the past tense so much is
possible.
       Old men should
learn to shut up.

There are other ways to be
than talk about it.

Waste is not good.
Waste is never kindly.

*

32.

I am not carried away
by poetry.

If a poem were to
carry me off, I'd say

put me down, we've
come a long way together.

Now tell me
what it was all about.

Oh, nothing. Nothing.

*

33.

If it is the nature of women
to scream, and men to shout
the rest, by right, is silence.

Snow drifting over our
forgiven names
whiting that human darkness.

I love the evening sunlight
north of the house. Her voice
from the kitchen calling me, come help.

Heaven is dry of blood. Air
fills the veins of the saved
whispering, mercy, mercy on us.

Such little breaths
from which the rain comes.

*

    34.

    the lovely irrecapturable
details. Dendrites
of snow adrift on air, becalmed
       like a leaf in ice.

Oktoberfest
       Boppard-am-Rhein '62
the innkeeper's wife said
       We do not take Jews here
(meant, but didn't say it)

Mutterland
     Vaterland
Arminius did for Varus
      in the Teutoburger Wald 9 A.D.
Panzers through winterforest in '44
     Your eyes
          Your hair
              Shulamit.

Downriver then
to hunt for shelter and food.

Down river, unforgiven
till love do us part.

*

35.

When a poem goes for a walk
it whistles up the neighbour's dog,
it breathes a thousand smells.

Tree, who are you
to tell me I'm not one.

Smoke over the river

Sun gone down.

*

36.

A hand raised
in greeting, or
to ward off the sun.

That, I say
is my brother. Walks

with the slow gait of a horse
or wind through the tall fieldgrass

across forty seven years

pencil marks
by the kitchen door

lengths of children
his years so much less.

*

37.

You came back that time
torn, a pale transparency

a fragment of life, light
a nuance, barely

Time steps across your eyes now
a pattern of mounting numbers
many as rain

You are ungathered history
Your name waits, waits
to be fingered, spoken.

Voice in a thimble, bone
sing me again
that reckless wild green song.

*

38.

First day of spring, I tell the grass.
Grass has the nerve
      to come back green.

Old discarded work-glove
full of gesture –
      not wind, not hand.

Owl takes flight at twilight.

Tranströmer:
      to row through
           the silence.

Syntax burns off as it speaks.

Poetry   the far nearness of rain.

*

    39.

Not an elegant war
this, as wars go. Spilt
blood smells ugly
      even onscreen.

The combed administrative suits
keep open mouths. They
mumble, for silence has
      an ugly sound.

Spilt, not over grass
or in dust, the blood, but
on cracked pavement
      that doesn't drink

but dries death up. Nothing
but the sun has
such thirst. Not even
      right and wrong.

*

    40.

Song –

as the wind rose
they talked just briefly

Are we responsible for
what we say.
              If so
why speak.

And the rain fell
and couldn't get up again.

Come to me now, he said.
I'm but a plain chest of drawers
built by a clumsy carpenter.

Song –
as the rain fell.

*

41.

Let a voice go and it
may run and hide.

Dry tears
of a lizard on a stone.

A poem, say, tragically in love
with a poem it has never met,

one that could release it
from the terrifying obligation to speak –

Together they might breed
new silences. Smell

water in the desert.
Wake with that hope.

*

    42.

It is a gift, this
green quiet of uncertainty
between words –

fertile speechlessness.

After before falls
the whole of time before
after recurs –
    a mask thrown high in the wind

lands where, or cannot
anywhere.
      A child
begins her song, and then forgets–

Such wide eyes of forgetting!

Who can think
this is not a loss

but a prize.

*

43.

A poem brought to light
returns to its darkness.
The remainder is words.

Grown old, you become
what you reach for,
can touch, without breaking.

Take beauty and
divide it into lines –
flute notes, a warbler's song

rises
      curves
            falls
scatters like rain off a tree.

Beauty is indivisible. The
remainder's an echo of light
in keeping with words.

*

44.

Here, there, memory fails
made up by threads of fiction.
Something must fill the holes

the spaces, the silence
so the fabric holds.

You are now my creation
as I am in part yours.
Stupidity, happiness, pain

we are one landscape,
where the light was once at home
but moved, has moved on –

wind above the mind, running, walking
the quick bodiless presence.

You, said the old one, and you,
join hands now. Be careful.

*

45.

Subject to object: sun wind rain
joined in ways language has
no hands for.

Words precede the unborn life –
hopes, fears, a name.

The homeless poem
grazes alone in some neighbour's field.
Lightyears are its substance.

It leaves no evidence
it was ever alive.

No soft prints in the snow.
No feather falls from the sky.

I am open
says the door.

*

    46.

The moon's phallic track across the water.
Munch's dispossessed lovers.
Summer's northern silence.

Not that things come and go
but are always there. One
earth, one century –

late or soon. The details multiply
that tell time. The opening
and closing of a hand. Two hands.

Once we had a house on a northern river.
Others now, no names left of that time.

Lovers dispossessed
become poems. That other silence.

*

47.

The word fingers contains
the word griefs
      the n left over wanders

join hands now.

Over whose body are you likely
to pray
      as a tree its shadow

knowing that, and that
      alone
is every season you own–

there –

breathtakingly –

*

48.

Say repetition is really
a recollecting forward

mutant cancer gene
in the family's blood

I thought I drank with the sun
but it was the moon, all along

the moon's
lovely long blood vowel

At the tomb of the unknown poem
they gather, intoning an ancient song

Orpheus   Orpheus

The words won't come.

*

49.

Not to
say something, but
to say
toward something, I think

says it.

In an hour the sun will rise.
There are no clouds.

Watch with me.

UNCOLLECTED POEMS

2008–2021

Breath

The full corn moon, then
first cool day of fall,
grey sky, quiet rain.

Something I forgot to say
or don't remember saying
taps at the window

asking
why no one comes
to let it in.

All the ferocity of history
is that one quiet touch
feathered to near-silence.

The burden is listening
long after the name has gone
your ear was home to.

Compassion

When walking with memory
go barefoot. Try
not to step
where the earth hurts.

A name mispronounced
can fell a tree.
Remember her soft first voice
before its weight leant on your arm.

Some are forgotten. We
are forgetful. The
ones we leave behind
watch us with startled eyes.

Autumnal

August scrap
to be cleared –
dead spiderwebs,
old mortgages.

Autumn is still a haze
settling in the eyes,
a step away. A friend

sends me a packet
of tiny fox teeth. I own
this ghostly creature now –

I run and hide.

On quiet nights
the stars know where I am.

Winter

The sun crosses my desk
making paper filigree shadows
of the stripped elm.

I remember, it says
everything I touch. A
terrible debt you owe me in little time.

My burnt hand strokes the chill out of your hair.
Now in the moon of the great cold
when the ponies grow their thick coats

your mind turns human , slow.
Your life's what passes for thanks.
I remember, I accept.

1918

I walked in through trees
birch, conifers, many kinds.
Evening curled me still.

This I remember.
Older shadows than the flight of birds
across the forested lake—

and in the atrium a fountain.
Wings filled with water.
Children playing.

At eleven the guns went silent.
At almost eleven almost all
the guns went silent.

Who can measure the silence of the guns.
The shadows of the trees the birds the lake.

And how cold it felt.

Western Light

The light that disappears.
A slow death, this
bleeding out of the sun.

To spend the night
in the arms of the great mulberry tree.
Climb back through the branches of a pine

above a hill
where someone sits who knows
the meaning of it all. Who's

neither alive, nor dead
but fated to be both. The
slit in the envelope

whose message is read.

Introit

The orphan is each of us.
You, no one gave name to.

He, or is it
she, his twin, a footprint thumb.

As the wind blows dust
pollen, seeds, us, on, on.

Let there be light
said the father. Or

to help you sleep
let the dark be absolute.

Birds

Crack their heads against
the glass we see through.

We mean you no harm.
Give us back our wings.

Quick life-prints in the snow.
Some of us make it home.

Past Tense

Sometimes, remotely, in dreams
he can hear the voices of memory singing

in the susurrus of snow falling
beyond the storm window.

I come from silence
and return to silence.

Who am I.
Who was that.

Notes on Poems

p. 258. 'Railroad Tracks, House for Sale and Clouds.' Title of a postcard I picked up in Quito, Ecuador.

p. 283 'Incarnations.' Most of the italicized lines are quotes from Roberto Calasso's fascinating exploration and retelling of the ancient myths of India, *Ka*. Corn Woman is Native American.

p. 289 'Apples and Apples.' Palestine here is the British Protectorate of the 1930s and '40s. The "she" of the poem and her family found haven there from European Fascism.

p. 306 'The Colour of Rocks, of Bread.' In her discussion of Nerval's sonnet 'El Desdichado,' Julia Kristeva notes that "ancholie" (an ingredient of "mélancolie") is French for the columbine flower, and this found its way into my poem. By chance, a few days after I'd finished the poem, the shootings occurred at Columbine High School in Colorado.

p. 317 'Departures.' The winter haiku is by Boncho, a friend and younger contemporary of Bashō. Reading it triggered a childhood memory.

p. 321 'New Year.' "I lift you from the river with my hands" is my interpretation of the pictograph meaning "help" (from *Indaba, My Children,* by Vusamazulu Credo Mutwa).

From the original book covers

Other Names for the Heart

In 1966, the Governor General's Award Committee selected Margaret Atwood's *The Circle Game* as the poetry prize winner. That decision marked the beginning of a decade or more of an almost pro-national emphasis in Canadian verse, an era in which influences from abroad, especially from British and European poetry, became markedly less noticeable. The other major contender for the 1966 Governor General's Award for Poetry was David Wevill's *A Christ of the Ice-Floes*.

Although he was born in Yokohama, Japan in 1935, was educated at Caius College, Cambridge and has lived and taught in Burma and Texas, David Wevill has remained steadfastly Canadian both in nationality and outlook. During the late Fifties and early Sixties he played a major role in "The Group" – a workshop and anthology – with such notable figures as George MacBeth, Peter Porter, Peter Redgrove, Alan Brownjohn, Zulfikar Ghose, Adrian Mitchell, Philip Hobsbaum and Edward Lucie-Smith. Wevill was also the only Canadian to be included in A. Alvarez's landmark anthology, *The New Poetry* (1965). It was from this period that Wevill's first two books emerged, *Birth of a Shark* (1964) and *A Christ of the Ice-Floes* (1966). These were followed by *Firebreak* (1971) and *Where the Arrow Falls* (1974).

Wevill has attempted to bring to his work the best of many different poetries: the terseness of Spanish language poets such as Lorca, Neruda, Machado and Paz; the meditative depth and strength of spirit found in Central and East European verse; the violent, often surreal perceptions of his British contemporaries; and the sharp, vibrant images that span the gap between life and death that link him to the essential canon of Canadian poetry.

With *Other Names for the Heart*, a book that chronicles the life and work of a compassionate survivor, David Wevill takes his rightful place among the best of Canada's poets. This selection of new and established work comes at a time when Canadian poetry stands again at a cross-roads – a time when our poets are preparing to enter the

community and continuum of world literature. As readers of *Other Names for the Heart* will discover, David Wevill has already carved his niche there.
—Bruce Meyer

Wevill's poetry is "varied, original, taut ... elaborate, skilful and very highly organized. All remarkably and convincingly his own."
—A. Alvarez

Figure of Eight

...*Figure of Eight* tells the tightly-woven story of a traveller seeking solace and understanding in the face of love and loss.

"Fine poems, in careful yet charged language, that meditate on a godless universe, on ancestral bonds with the desert, on age and death ... a lyrical ear and a rueful sense of the limits of the lives we build."
Books in Canada

Solo With Grazing Deer

David Wevill has lived in England, Burma, Spain and currently makes his home in Texas. *Books in Canada* has said: "Careful yet charged language, that meditates on a godless universe, on ancestral bonds, on age and death."

Asterisks

The poems here step out of the silence, speak briefly, and step back again. They have no names. They are moments in time, asterisks, images or signs that refer us to somewhere else in memory or time, that remains still hidden.

www.ingramcontent.com/pod-product-compliance
Lightning Source LLC
Chambersburg PA
CBHW031750220426
43662CB00007B/343